The
Word-A-Day
Vocabulary Builder

The
Word-A-Day
Vocabulary Builder

Bergen Evans

with a foreword by

Jess Stein

Editorial Director Emeritus
Random House Dictionaries

Ballantine Books • New York

The
Word-A-Day
Vocabulary Builder

Library of Congress Catalog Card Number: 63-18714

ISBN 0-345-30610-4

This edition published by arrangement with Random House, Inc.

Manufactured in the United States of America

First Ballantine Books Edition: August 1982

FOREWORD

by *Jess Stein*
Editorial Director Emeritus
Random House Dictionaries

*T*his book is an extremely effective guide to increasing your vocabulary. Based on several decades of experience by one of America's finest teachers, it will help you add clarity and power to your speech and writing by a technique that is natural, practical, and—in the best sense —habit-forming.

You can expect many valuable benefits from the improvement of your vocabulary: You will understand more exactly what others are saying or writing. You will be able to express yourself with greater clarity and effectiveness. You will be able to think more clearly and sort out ideas more precisely. And you will find that you enjoy, as a result, greater self-confidence in human relations.

Bergen Evans begins this book by increasing your awareness of language generally and then discussing the nature and history of the English language. Once you have this foundation, you proceed to the study of individual words. But, in the end, you will have acquired more than just new words—you will have gained a special insight into language and the lifetime ability to keep improving the range and effectiveness of your vocabulary.

Follow the suggestions below and you will soon have many new words at your command, some mainly for your recognition vocabulary and others for your active speaking and writing vocabulary.

First, select one word a day from this book and write it on a small card. Study the word in spare moments during the day— its meaning, spelling, pronunciation—and try to form sentences that use it. Don't try to do more than a word a day.

Second, during the course of the day, when you encounter any unfamiliar words, write them on the back of the card. Find their meanings in your dictionary and be sure you learn their spelling and pronunciation as well —make them yours. Develop the dictionary habit.

Using the method of this book, you will build a vocabulary in relationship to *your own individual needs and interests*.

CONTENTS

1

The Importance of an Effective Vocabulary

Speech our most important tool . . . Misunderstandings due to words . . . Need for larger vocabulary . . . Pleasures of well-chosen words . . . Increased vocabulary makes learning easier . . . Difficulty of finding the exact word . . . Vocabulary shapes decisions . . . Words and prejudice . . . Vocabulary and intelligence.

Words are the tools for the job of saying what you want to say. And what you want to say are your thoughts and feelings, your desires and your dislikes, your hopes and your fears, your business and your pleasure—almost everything, indeed, that makes up *you*. Except for our vegetablelike growth and our animallike impulses, almost all that we are is related to our use of words. Humanity has been defined as a tool-using animal, but its most important tool, the one that distinguishes human beings from all other animals, is speech.

As with other tools, the number and variety of the words we know should meet all our needs. Not than anyone has ever had a vocabulary exactly fitted to his or her every need at all times. The greatest writers—those who have shown the rest of us how *in*adequate our own command of words is—have agonized over their verbal shortcomings. But we can approach our needs. The more words we know, the closer we can come to expressing precisely what we want to.

We can, for instance, give clear instructions, and reduce misunderstandings. If we say, "See that he does it," we should make sure that the person spoken to knows what he is to do when he *sees*, that it is clear to him who *he* is and what *it* is and what must be accomplished to *do* it.

1

Some of history's great disasters have been caused by misunderstood directions. The heroic but futile charge of the Light Brigade at Balaclava in the Crimean War is a striking example. "Someone had blundered," Tennyson wrote. That was true, and the blunder consisted of the confusion over one word, which meant one thing to the person speaking but another to the persons spoken to.

The brigade was ordered to charge "the guns." The man who gave the order was on a hilltop and had in mind a small battery which was very plain to him but was concealed from the soldiers in the valley by a slight rise. The only guns *they* could see were the main Russian batteries at the far end of the valley. Therefore they assumed that "the guns" referred to the batteries *they* saw. The command seemed utter madness, but it was a command and the leader of the Brigade after filing a protest, carried it out.

Fortunately, most misunderstandings don't have such disastrous consequences. But the continual confusion about such general terms as *thing, deal, it, fix,* and the like, certainly can be frustrating. Taken as a whole, the exasperation, humiliation, disappointment and quarreling caused by misunderstandings probably produce a thousand times the misery and suffering that the Light Brigade endured.

So the wise person, who wants peace of mind, and the efficient person, who wants to get on with the job, will take the trouble to use specific terms instead of doubtful ones.

Besides clarity, a large vocabulary provides variety. And that is useful; it is the basis for discrimination, since it provides a larger number of tools to choose from. A hammer won't do when a file is called for. Furthermore, a large and varied vocabulary makes the speaker or writer more interesting. It allows him or her to avoid the dullness of repetition and to provoke attention. The interesting person is much more likely to be persuasive than the dull one. Dull people bore us. We don't listen to them. We hear them, but with a secret distaste. Instead of listening to them, we think only about getting away from them. Therefore a varied vocabulary is very useful for winning others to our point of view.

Thomas Wolfe reveled in words with more glory and gusto than perhaps anyone since Shakespeare or Rabelais. On seeing a shabby little man lying dead on a subway bench, Wolfe was struck with the thought of the dull and miserable existence such a man must have had because of the sterility of his speech. "Poor, dismal, ugly, sterile, shabby little man," Wolfe wrote in his essay,

"Death the Proud Brother," "with your little scrabble of harsh oaths, and cries, and stale constricted words, your pitiful little designs and feeble purposes.... Joy, glory, and magnificence were here for you upon this earth, but you scrabbled along the pavements rattling a few stale words like gravel in your throat, and would have none of them."

When Caliban, the half-human monster in Shakespeare's last play, *The Tempest*, furiously denies that he owes any gratitude to his master, the magician Prospero, he demands to know what Prospero has ever done for him. The magician passes over all the many benefits he has conferred on the wretched creature, to stress only one: he has taught him to speak.

> *I... took pains to make thee speak.*
> *When thou didst not, savage,*
> *Know thine own meaning, but wouldst gabble like*
> *A thing most brutish, I endow'd thy purposes*
> *With words that made them known.*

The simple fact is that we all begin as Calibans—and do not know even our own purposes until we endow them with words. Do not, indeed, know ourselves. The pleasure you will feel as you develop your vocabulary is not solely the pleasure that comes with increased power; it is also the greater pleasure that comes with increased knowledge, especially of yourself. You will begin to appreciate expression as an art and to feel not only the advantage of commanding words but the satisfaction. You will notice that this or that phrase which someone utters in your hearing or which you see in the newspapers is very good.

And you will be pleased that it *is* good, just as you are pleased to see a forward pass completed, or a long putt holed, or a dance step gracefully executed. For words are to the mind what such actions are to the body.

You will see that the rightness of a well-chosen word is not merely a source of pleasure; it may provoke the most serious consequences or avoid the gravest danger. When, for example, America and Russia confronted each other during the Cuban crisis in 1962, and the world hovered for a few days on the brink of disaster, the use of the word *quarantine* instead of *blockade* was extremely important. A *blockade* is an act of war. No one knew quite what a *quarantine* meant, under the circumstances. But the very use of the word indicated that, while we were determined to protect ourselves, we wanted to avoid war. It was all a part of giving Russia some possibility of saving face. We wanted her missiles and planes out of Cuba and were prepared to fight even a nuclear war to get them out. But we certainly preferred to have them removed peacefully. We did not want to back Russia into a corner from which there could have been no escape except by violence.

Thus the use of *quarantine*, a purposefully vague word, was part of our strategy. Furthermore, it had other advantages over *blockade*. It is commonly associated with a restriction imposed by all civilized nations on people with certain communicable diseases to prevent them from spreading their disease throughout the community. It is a public health measure which, for all the inconvenience that it may impose on the afflicted individual, serves the public welfare. Thus, whereas a *blockade* would have been an announcement that we were proceeding aggressively to further our own interests, regardless of the rights of others, *quarantine* suggested a concern for the general welfare. In addition, it suggested that what was going on in Cuba was a dangerous disease which might easily spread.

So, as you develop a larger vocabulary you will be increasingly aware of what is going on. You will enjoy what you read more. New pleasures will be opened to you.

You will understand more. Difficult books whose meaning has been uncertain will become readable. The great poets who have enlarged our experience, the philosophers who have shaped our thoughts, the historians who have sought for patterns in the human story, the essayists whose observations have delighted people for centuries—all these and more will be available to you. And in sharing their thoughts your own world will expand. This particular benefit of an increased vocabulary is dramatically apparent in the strides that children make in comprehension as they progress in their use of language. Increased learning increases the child's word stock and the increased word stock makes learning easier. The National Conference on Research in English says "a child's ability to read, to speak, to write, and to think is inevitably conditioned by his vocabulary."

This goes for an adult too. Words cannot be separated from ideas. They interact. The words we use are so associated with our experiences and what the experiences mean to us that they cannot be separated. The idea comes up from our subconscious clothed in words. It can't come any other way.

We don't know how words are stored in our minds, but there does seem to be a sort of filing system. The filing system appears to be controlled by a perverse if not downright wacky filing clerk. Everyone has tried to remember a word and been unable to. Sometimes it is a common word, one that we *know* we know. Yet it won't come when we want it. It can be almost a form of torture trying to recall it, but no amount of fuming or fretting helps. Then suddenly, usually some time later when it is no longer useful to us, it will come to mind readily. When we are searching for one of these words—often for a person's name—we will come up with other words or names that we know are close to but not exactly the one we want. This is curious in itself. For if we can't remember the word we want, how do we know the other word is very much like it? It's as though the filing clerk had seen the word we actually wanted or was even holding it in his hand but wouldn't give it to us.

Often we know that the unacceptable word has the same sound or begins with the same letter as the word we can't remember. And when we finally recall the word we wanted, we find this is so. It seems as though our mental filing systems were arranged alphabetically and cross-indexed for similarity of internal sound. If we are well-read, we can call up a host of synonyms (words that mean the same thing) for many words, which suggests more cross-filing. Furthermore, words have subtle and complex associations. The speech and writing of some people who have sustained brain injuries or suffered strokes indicate a curious kind of damage. Some injured people seem to lose all proper names, some all adjectives, and many mix capitals and small letters. This indicates that the interlocking connections of words in our minds are more complex than we can imagine. The chances are that the most spectacular computer is a simple gadget compared to the human mind.

For our purposes, our ignorance of how this intricate filing system works does not matter. What matters to a person trying to enlarge his vocabulary is the many connections among the words he knows. Once we master the word, it is connected in our mind with scores of other words in what appears to be an infinite number of relationships and shades of meaning. A new word does not drop as a single addition into our word stock. Each new word learned enlarges a whole complex of thinking and is itself enlarged in meaning and significance.

A vocabulary is a tool which one uses in formulating the important questions of life, the questions which must be asked before they can be answered. To a large extent, vocabulary shapes all the decisions we make. Most decisions, of course, are shaped by our emotions, by circumstances, and by the forces which may hold us back or urge us on. These circumstances and forces are largely beyond our control. But our speech is a sort of searchlight that helps us to see these things more clearly and to see ourselves in relation to them. At least it helps us call things by their right names.

To a great extent our speech affects our judgments. We don't always—sometimes we can't—distinguish between words and things. A slogan, for example, especially if it rhymes, or is alliterative (that is, has a number of words that begin with the same sound), or has a strong rhythm, will move us to action. It convinces us that the action is necessary. "Motorists wise Simoniz" is far more effective in promoting sales than "Simoniz, wise motorists" or "Wise motorists, Simoniz" would have been. It's the witchery of rhythm, one of the most subtle and danger- ous of unseen forces that move and muddle our minds. Seduced by "Fifty-four forty or fight," our great-grandfathers almost went to war in 1844. And there are historians who trace much of the misery of the modern world to the fascination that Grant's "Unconditional surrender" held for four generations of Americans.

Certainly anyone who develops the valuable habit of examin- ing his or her own prejudices will find that many of them are, at bottom, verbal. A situation automatically calls forth a single word. The word is bathed in emotion. So whenever the situation is repeated, it produces the same emotional response. There is no effort to be rational, to see what is actually going on. The word triggers the response. But the more words one has at one's command, the greater the possibility that one may be one's own master. It takes words to free us from words. Removing an emotionally charged word from a phrase and substituting a neutral synonym often gives us an insight that nothing else can.

Speech is the means of relating our separate experiences and emotions, of combining them, reliving them and, as far as we can, understanding them. If we did not have the words *justice*, *equal*, *radiation*—and a thousand others like them—our minds and our whole lives would be much narrower. Each new word of this kind increases the scope of thought and adds its bit to humanity. Once we have the word, of course, it seems natural and it is an effort to imagine being without it.

Consider that remarkable British phrase which Lord Broughton invented during the reign of George IV (1820-1830): "His Majesty's opposition." Political parties rose in seventeenth- century England during a period of limited civil war and they behaved as if parliamentary victories were military ones. When one party gained power it immediately proceeded to impeach the leaders of the other party, demanding their very heads. But after a hundred and fifty years of peace and prosperity, men's tempers began to cool. A sense of fairness compelled them to grant their neighbor the right to a different opinion and even to grant that those who opposed them might still be loyal and honorable. But the atmosphere Lord Broughton described had to precede his phrase, just as the invention of the wheel had to precede the medieval concept of Fortune's wheel.

Once uttered, the phrase helped to further the idea it described. People saw that criticism of an administration could be as much a part of good government as the government itself and that a person was not necessarily a traitor because he or she disagreed with the party in power.

Many studies have established the fact that there is a high correlation between vocabulary and intelligence and that the ability to increase one's vocabulary throughout life is a sure reflection of intellectual progress.

It is hard to stretch a small vocabulary to make it do all the things that intelligent people require of words. It's like trying to plan a series of menus from the limited resources of a poverty-stricken, war-torn country compared to planning such a series in a prosperous, stable country. Words are one of our chief means of adjusting to all the situations of life. The better control we have over words, the more successful our adjustment is likely to be.

2

Sizes And Kinds Of Vocabularies

Growth of English language...Words we know vs. those we use...Inferring the meaning from the context...Each occupation and situation has special vocabularies...2,000 spoken words vs. 15,000 to 100,000 reading vocabulary...570 words with 7,000 uses...The search for basic vocabularies...Burns, Shakespeare, Milton...How to expand vocabulary...Don't guess at meanings.

No one knows for sure how many words there are in the language or how many there were in the past. We are not certain how many words anyone knows. We're not even sure just what *knowing* a word means.

It would seem simple to estimate how many Old English words there were, since there is a limited body of Old English literature and very little likelihood of any more being discovered. But estimates of the written vocabulary run from 37,000 to 60,000. Since these can be made only from what was written down, the size of the spoken vocabulary can only be a matter of opinion. Some have put the upper limit at 100,000. But if that is accurate, then an extraordinarily high percentage of the entire speech managed to get itself into a fairly small body of specialized literature.

The estimates for Middle English (the period lasting from about 1150 to 1400 A.D.) range from 50,000 to 125,000 words. We think the spoken vocabulary in Shakespeare's day consisted of about 140,000 words.

Dictionaries began to appear in the seventeenth century, but they don't help in the estimates very much, because the early ones made no pretense of including the entire vocabulary. It was not until the late nineteenth century that comprehensiveness became an aim of lexicography. The earliest (Cawdrey's, 1604) listed only "hard words" and only 3,000 of those. Kersey's, early in the eighteenth century, selected words most commonly used and had 35,000 of them. Dr. Johnson's famous dictionary (1755) had 40,000, though the same year the Scott-Bailey dictionary included 65,000.

In the United States, Noah Webster's 1806 dictionary included about 37,000 words, but his 1828 dictionary had about 70,000. *The Century Dictionary*, which was planned in 1882 and first appeared in 1889, had about 200,000, approximately 120,000 more than had appeared in any English dictionary up to that time. And by 1911, the editors found it necessary to add 100,000 more.

Estimates of the present word stock of English run from half a million to over a million, depending on whether one counts only roots (like *go*) or all forms of the verb (*went, gone, going*), whether one counts all irregular plurals (*feet, sheep,* etc.) as separate words, and so on.

On one thing, however, the counters are in complete agreement. The increasing complexity of life along with rapid technological development have led to a fast increase in the number of words at our disposal. More new words were added to English between 1850 and 1950 in the field of chemistry alone than Old English acquired from all sources in five hundred years. On the basis of the trend since 1600 (a date arbitrarily chosen to mark the end of the period of Shakespearian English and the beginning of that of Modern English), we can expect our vocabulary to double in the next two centuries.

This suggests that a larger vocabulary will be expected of the individual, but there will probably be an increasing gap between the individual vocabulary and the total number of words in the language. Increasingly, every profession and occupation is acquiring a special vocabulary, and very few people need to know more than one of these.

Or at least to know how to use more than one. When we speak of *knowing* a word, we employ a disturbingly vague term. One study explains it as "the ability to define a term in one's own words, giving the gist of any accepted meaning, or illustrating a proper use of a word in a sentence so as to demonstrate a useful knowledge of its meaning."

One difficulty in the way of estimating the number of words anyone *knows* is that we all have several levels of vocabulary or even several vocabularies. With our families and close friends, on the ordinary unimportant occasions of daily life, we speak much of the time in grunts and monosyllables. Although we leave many words out of our sentences, the other person knows what we're talking about, knows what certain words mean to us. It would be not only unnecessary but pompous to round out our sentences. Nothing will stir up resentment in the bosom of the family more quickly than showing off with formal, complete sentences.

When dealing with strangers, however, in our business or profession, we will be more formal, round out our sentences, use words that would seem stiff at home. At home we may show agreement by grunting "Yup" or "Yeah" or "Okay" or "Okeydoke." But when we are being interviewed for a job, we say "Yes" or "Certainly." And when the boss asks whether we agree with an opinion he has just expressed with great feeling, we will say, "Sir, I find myself not only in eager agreement with the sentiment so brilliantly expressed but awestruck at the sagacity which conceived it." Or something like that.

In addition, we are able to read or hear with full understanding and even enjoyment a literary language or the language of public speaking or diplomacy, but we would hesitate to use it. For instance, most of us use *I guess* to indicate that we do not have absolute knowledge about something. We all know the word *assume*. We might even use it at home and would think nothing of using or hearing it away from home. We would also understand *conjecture* just as clearly as we understand *guess*, but we would not use it very often. So too with *surmise*. Most people would understand *postulate*, but if they heard it in any but very formal circumstances, they would think it rather highfalutin. They would be inclined to resent it or to snicker. *Posit* would simply bewilder most people, though after a few seconds they would *know* it. *Methinks* would be understood at once. We would accept it if we heard it on the stage in a play that we knew was old. But on any other occasion, we would regard it as unnatural, facetious, or intolerably affected.

So from just listening to our talk, it would be misleading to assume that because we invariably use *guess*, we do not know any other words. We know a dozen, even though we would use only one or two of them. And we know their many different shades of meaning and appropriate uses.

There are many words whose meaning may be inferred from the contexts in which they appear, even the first time we see them. If we read that "on cold or rainy days the airplane is towed into the hangar to be repaired," it is plain that a hangar must be some sort of covered structure large enough to hold an airplane. Or when we read in Thomas Fuller's *Worthies of England* (1662) that officers of the city of London "claimed a privilege to themselves to garble the live pigs in the markets of the city," it is plain that *garble* must have had some meaning in 1662 that it doesn't have three hundred years later. And when Fuller continues that "such as they found starved or otherwise unwholesome for man's sustenance they would slit in the ear and turn them loose," we realize, however much it may astonish us, that *garble* once meant to sort the good from the bad, picking and choosing.

One authority believes that for every word in constant use in our speech, ten more could be recognized and even used if necessary. For everyone recognizes words he or she never uses in speaking, either through context or by familiarity with the root.

The colloquial language of one's everyday conversation does not necessarily reflect the formal vocabulary of one's writing. And the requirements of particular situations might evoke words, in speech or writing, which would surprise the speaker's associates. A farmer might know many terms unfamiliar to a city dweller. Regional and particularly rural speech can have both a humor and a dignity which is not to be found in conventional urban language.

So although we recognize that there are many levels of vocabulary, there is no satisfactory way of measuring what proportion of any individual's vocabulary belongs in any specific category. One authority has estimated that two thousand words, thoroughly understood and available, are enough for ordinary conversation. A fairly good reading vocabulary, the same authority guesses, would require fifteen thousand.

There is a great range of estimates on how large a vocabulary is employed at different ages and education levels. Some students of the subject once concluded that a child entering school would have about twenty-five hundred words, a stupid adult ten thousand, and an average adult from thirty-five to seventy thousand. But a study made by Professor Robert Seashore at Northwestern University a few years ago suggested that children used and recognized many more words than had been supposed. On the basis of evidence that Professor Seashore had accumulated in repeated tests, he felt that the average child added about five thousand new basic and derivative words to his vocabulary every year. This was about ten times the number that had previously been assumed. Seashore concluded that first-graders might have as many as sixteen thousand words in their vocabularies and that the average university student would have between sixty thousand and a hundred thousand. Since then other studies have borne him out.

From the very beginning of the study of vocabularies, investigators were convinced that under all individual, regional, and occupational variations there was a common stock of words, suitable for all occasions and shared by all users of the language. As early as 1588, Timothy Bright, who invented a sort of shorthand, selected a list of 559 words which he felt were basic and universal in English.

In the twentieth century, the search for a basic vocabulary has occupied many students of education. Their purpose was to determine what we should teach children in order to give them an adequate control of the language. E. L. Thorndike's influential study produced the Thorndike teacher's word books. Thorndike compiled these books from millions of words actually used in printing or in speech by counting the number of times each word was used in every thousand spoken or written. Ernest Horn—and many others—conducted similar studies.

They all showed that most vocabularies are made up of a fairly small number of words (approximately two thousand) which are used most of the time (approximately ninety percent of the time). An individual draws on the larger resources of his or her vocabulary only occasionally.

A moment's thought about our own speech habits will confirm this. We use the word *get*, let us say, ten times for every once that we use *obtain* or *procure*.

And we have many meanings for the common words. Such words as *fix* and *do* will have scores of meanings in our speech, but the more formal, less-used words are more specialized and therefore not as helpful as general tools. In a supplement to Thorndike's work, one of his colleagues, Irving Lorge, found that the 570 commonest words had 7,000 different uses. The word with the most meanings was *run*. *Put, make, work* and *stand* followed.

Such lists have been extremely influential in selecting words for children's textbooks, stories, and spelling lists. Many educators feel they should be used as the basis for a minimum required vocabulary, with the possibility of requiring a knowledge of 15,000 words for high school graduation.

But although a good vocabulary is highly desirable—and a sizeable vocabulary might be a better requirement for high school graduation than some of the current requirements—it is hard to believe that people could ever agree on a definite list.

This doesn't mean, of course, that the vocabulary of an illiterate is superior to the vocabulary of a learned person. Overall, the learned person is able to say more things (and say them well) than is the illiterate. Dr. Johnson observed that the speech of the uneducated is sufficient to their thoughts and interests, because their thoughts and interests are narrow. The chances are that the poet Robert Burns didn't have a peasant's vocabulary at all, but that he used a peasant's words for a poet's purposes. Still, his use of peasant speech to express sentiments which later generations in different circumstances and different lands have recognized as their own most intimate experiences does show that a fixed, uniform vocabulary would more likely be an impoverishment than an enrichment. No one list of required words could possibly meet all needs. It is far better that out of the great mass of words available to us, along with a small, basic shared number, each can select his own.

Estimates have been made of the vocabularies of a number of great writers. But we have no way of knowing what a dead author's actual vocabulary was. All we can count are the words used in his or her writing. Until quite recently, most of the words one used every day were not considered quite fit for the loftier purposes of writing. Shakespeare's vocabulary has been estimated at from 15,000 to 24,000 words. But there are many words which we know were common in his day (such as *blunders, decency, delicacy, existence*) which don't appear in his plays or poems. Shakespeare undoubtedly knew these words and used them in his speech, but they can't be listed in any count of his vocabulary.

Milton's poetry yields about 8,000 words. But that doesn't tell us as much about Milton's vocabulary as it does about the dangers of such lists. For as we have noted, 8,000 is about the working vocabulary of an ordinary second-grader. One doesn't have to know much Milton or many second-graders to realize that his command of language would startle any second-grade teacher out of his wits. We know also that many words occur in Milton's prose that do not appear in his poetry. He used such a small number of words because his poetry and prose dealt with very special subjects in a very special way. And that called for a very special vocabulary.

There are various ways of extending the vocabulary. And we all practice the main ones—reading and talking—every day. But if we talk to the same people about the same subjects—as most of us do—and read the same papers and magazines year in and year out, we will soon come to a point of diminishing returns.

The exceptional man, say, who wants to enlarge his speech and his thoughts and to express himself more effectively will make a conscious effort to break out of a deadly routine. When he encounters a totally strange word, he will look it up; when he finds, as he usually will, several meanings ascribed to it, he will give some thought to the context of the word. When he meets a strange word that he thinks he understands from the context, he will still look it up—just to make sure that his assumption was correct. He will often find that it was *not*. He may discover that the word has meanings he had not suspected. One of these meanings might show the passage to have a meaning different from the one he had assumed. In this case, he should not feel let down because his guess was wrong, but elated because he was right not to let his guesses go unchecked.

One way of breaking out of a routine is by using a book like this. By mastering a new word every day, by being continually on the alert for it in conversation and reading, by using it with discretion in one's own speech, the exceptional person will, if only by heightened awareness of words and meanings, move himself or herself up into a wholly different intellectual class.

3

Appropriateness vs. Size

*Meeting individual needs... Words must be familiar
...Appropriate vocabularies...Jargon...Limits of Basic
English...A more effective vocabulary...Embarassing
words... Plain and unusual words... Precise choice of words.*

A large vocabulary is not necessarily a good vocabulary. In their masterpieces, the great users of the language have often employed surprisingly few words. Any government bulletin, military directive, postal instruction, or interoffice memo will contain far more strange words than are to be found in the Twenty-third Psalm, Hamlet's soliloquy, or any one of our hundred best lyrical poems.

The best vocabulary is the one which most effectively meets the needs of the individual. And the needs of the individual depend on his or her nature, background, environment, and on the situation immediately confronting that person.

There is an amusing illustration of this in James Boswell's *Account of Corsica* (1768). Boswell, who was later to write the *Life of Samuel Johnson*, the greatest biography ever written, was a curious and adventurous man. His inquisitiveness and sense of adventure led him, when he was very young, to the island of Corsica. He was searching for Pascal Paoli, the leader of a revolt against the Genoese, who claimed to own the island. Corsica is a wild place today. It was then even wilder, inhabited by bandits and torn with a murderous revolutionary war and numerous blood feuds and vendettas. As Boswell was riding into the mountainous interior of the island, he was suddenly surrounded by a fierce-looking gang. They sprang out of the underbrush and seized his horse's bridle, swearing and threatening him. They demanded to know who he was and what he wanted in those parts. Their tone of voice left no doubt that unless satisfactory answers were forthcoming at once, he would be killed. Then and there.

Boswell told them that he was an Englishman and that he was seeking their chieftain to pay him his respects. The second part of this statement put him in a good light, but the first filled the bandits with horror. For Englishmen, they had heard, were heretics and should not be allowed to live. The leader fiercely demanded why Boswell was not a Catholic. Boswell, either paralyzed with terror or gifted with a brilliant hunch, said that England was too far from Rome. The brigands thought this over, decided it was a very reasonable excuse for heresy, and let him go on his way.

Now as an explanation for religion, Boswell's excuse was absurd. As a plea for his life, it was pitiful. But as a means of getting himself out of a dangerous situation, it was highly effective. All the fancy words in the world would not have served him better, and the chances are that using even a few would have cost him his life. The situation he was in called for the unhesitating expression of a very simple thought in very simple words. Luckily for him, that's what he came up with.

That doesn't mean simple words are *always* the best. The Gettysburg Address, for example, is not written in completely simple language. "Four score and seven" is not as simple as "eighty-seven," "brought forth" is more old-fashioned than "established," and "dedicated to the proposition" sounds clumsy. Yet the overall effect of that great oration lies in its gloomy magnificence. And that is just what *that* occasion needed. The North knew that it had won a great victory at Gettysburg and was rejoicing. But it was horrified at the enormous price in life and treasure it had already paid and might yet pay again. And thousands were numb with grief and despair at the death of their sons.

The brevity of the Address was in itself a master stroke. The crowd had already listened for two hours to Dr. Edward Everett, generally regarded as the greatest orator of the age. It was an age that could absorb a lot of oratory. Even so, the audience must have been worn out when the learned rhetorician gave way to the former backwoodsman.

Whether three minutes later they knew that they had heard one of the greatest speeches of all time, we don't know. And it doesn't matter. They knew that they had heard the right thing, that the President had said exactly what should have been said.

We are told that the Address was received in silence, which was probably the highest tribute to its effectiveness and appropriateness. It was not a time for applause. The rich language, though unnecessary just to express his ideas, lent Lincoln's speech the dignity the occasion demanded. The slightly old-fashioned language and biblical rhythms must have called forth echoes of the Bible that moved his hearers' minds to the comforts of religion.

The most famous phrase in the speech—"Government of the people, by the people, for the people"—was not original. Several others had expressed the idea publicly on previous occasions, one of them very near to the time of the Address. But the very fact that the idea, so expressed, was in the air may have helped. It may have made Lincoln's phrase seem sound, established, indisputable, even homely, "altogether fitting." And that is what a funeral oration should be. It's no occasion for wit and brilliance.

The ordinary man, of course, is not often called on to justify his religion with a dagger at his throat or to eulogize the dead after a great victory. His life is not often at stake, and millions rarely hang with eager expectation upon his every syllable. His meaning *is* often at stake. Achievement or frustration may hang in the balance, and pride and reputation may be affected. And all by a man's use of words.

So we must have words. But the mere accumulation of them won't do much good. They must be so familiar to us, respond so well to our needs that our speech draws them automatically from our minds. We don't often have time to stop and think, to select the exact word. Yet if we are to achieve even our most commonplace objectives, we have to *use* the right word. And that means that the right word must be a habit. It must come naturally when we need it.

A large vocabulary, like a great deal of learning, may actually be a source of confusion. It may blur meanings and misdirect attention. Everett prefaced what *he* had to say at Gettysburg with an account of the funerary customs of the ancient Greeks. It was very learned and most impressive, but the world noted it very little and didn't remember it very long.

A large, specialized vocabulary is obviously useful in its own area. A scientist, for instance, communicates with colleagues in terms which would be meaningless to a lay person. Some of this is necessary. The scientist must have words that are free of the emotional and historical overtones of most everyday words. But much of it is mere jargon to make the particular knowledge seem greater than it is, or to make the people who use it seem like a special group. And it has long been noted that the very great men and women in many highly specialized fields can make themselves understood to lay people better than some of their less important colleagues.

The use of a specialized vocabulary outside of professional activities is a handicap, not an asset. For instance, in the course of treating a patient, a doctor may say that a certain medicine is *indicated*, meaning that it is needed. But if he drove into a gas station and said that twenty gallons of gas was indicated, he would either be misunderstood or laughed at.

Such a thing isn't likely, of course. We all have several vocabularies and select our words from the one that we think is appropriate to the circumstances and the company. We don't stop and select it, as we would select a tie from a rack in a store or an item from a menu. We would be tongue-tied or stammering if we did. But we do it all the same. We do it unconsciously only because we have tested our words repeatedly in every kind of company and know without thinking the meaning they will convey and the effect they will have.

Of course, no speaker is ever absolutely certain about the effect he or she will have: Response is a highly conditioned matter. For example, an entertainer who has always gotten a laugh with a harmless joke about a bankruptcy may have the misfortune to repeat it in a community where the failure of a local firm has just caused widespread unemployment. To his amazement, the joke will elicit anger instead of applause. We have all had similar experiences, though usually with a smaller audience.

If our scientist happened to be one who did a good deal of lecturing and writing to popularize some subject, he or she would have to have a general vocabulary to match the professional vocabulary. A lecturer cannot catch the interest of a nonprofessional audience—or even of a single listener—with a special vocabulary that the audience can't understand. It will just make them feel inferior, resentful, and angry. To hold our interest on any subject in which we do not have a direct material or emotional interest, a style must have variety, precision, and flexibility. These can come only from a word stock rich enough to provide the exact word for the occasion and to provide synonyms to avoid the dullness of repetition.

It is possible to get on with a limited vocabulary. But anyone who does is restricted to simple thoughts and experiences. His or her expression is neither graceful nor subtle. Such a person must be content with approximations rather than with exact statements and expect that the meaning is more likely to be guessed at than clearly understood.

For instance, Basic English has just 850 words, of which only eighteen are verbs. It might conceivably be suitable for some simple business transaction. But all precision and subtlety would have to be sacrificed. The many well-known writings which have been translated into Basic show what it is capable of. But while these translations have proved that the main outline of almost any simple statement can be conveyed in Basic, they have also shown that conciseness, grace, flexibility—most of what makes communication between human beings pleasurable— must be sacrificed.

Basic English does not prove that a simple vocabulary is enough. It simply suggests that people who cannot speak English could probably make do at the most elementary level with a simple store of words. But no one whose native speech is English could ever function within the limitations of Basic. Before one could even understand what Basic was, one would, of necessity, know many hundreds of words outside of Basic that were more suitable for particular occasions than the Basic word. On such occasions it would be practically impossible to keep one's mind from selecting them.

The aim of vocabulary study should be to increase the *effective* vocabulary. Merely to add to the number of words one knows superficially does no good. The chances are that it will lead to misuse and ridicule. Take the old joke of the foreigner who said that he and his wife had no children because she was "unbearable." This illustrates the pitfall into which we all may stumble when we use a word whose meaning, or one of whose several meanings, we have grasped imperfectly. For instance, if one knows the common word *repulsive*, one may easily acquire its synonym *repellent*. But there are times when they are not synonymous, and when using them interchangeably could be embarrassing. It would not be the compliment one intended to tell a friend that his new water-repellent topcoat was repulsive.

One has to know all the potentialities of a given word—or at least all that are current—to avoid such disasters or to speak with the directness and clarity that gain attention. Effective communication does not depend on a vocabulary of long words or a vocabulary of small words. It depends on an easy familiarity with the right words—that is, words immediately understood in their context, precisely expressing the speaker's thought and feeling, and received by the hearer with the effects intended.

Everyone knows someone who loves to show off a large vocabulary, even to the point of becoming a standing joke in the community. Dickens portrayed one of the more lovable of this breed in Mr. Wilkins Micawber in *David Copperfield*. " 'Under the impression,' said Mr. Micawber, 'that your peregrinations in this metropolis have not as yet been extensive, and that you might have some difficulty in penetrating the arcana of the modern Babylon ... in short,' said Mr. Micawber in a burst of confidence, 'that you might lose your way ...' " The world has laughed good-naturedly at Mr. Micawber for a hundred years, but it's easy to be good-natured towards fools in fiction. The response to real fools is not always so kind.

But simple, familiar language, though safer, is not always the most appropriate either. Sir Ernest Gowers, a very lively authority on the use of words, cites Sir Winston Churchill as a man who knows how to use the plain *and* the unusual effectively. Thus, Gowers points out, in the first volume of his history of the Second World War, Sir Winston uses the unusual word *flocculent* instead of the more common *woolly* to describe the fuzzy-mindedness of certain people. The choice was excellent because *woolly*, although better understood, has lost its effect through overuse. It is ordinary, neutral, and, worst of all, sounds slightly irritable. It suggests that the fuzzy-minded ones were at least important enough to have been irritating. Whereas *flocculent*, though it has the same basic meaning as woolly, is, by its very unusualness, striking. And Churchill's deliberate choice of a slightly pompous synonym shows that he is joking, that *flocculent* people only amuse him. *Flocculent*, in this context, conveys contempt and, if there is any irritation, conceals it under a jest.

Thus not only did Sir Winston convey his exact meaning (woolly, with all its associations of spongy softness, snarled confusion, lack of a definite thread) but his exact emotional attitude (contempt tinged with good humor) and, at the same time, protected himself against charges of irritability and ill humor.

And all this by using one word instead of another that meant the same thing!

4

The English Language

The most widely used language... The origins of English ...Borrowed words... How language changes... "Foreign" words added to English... Standard ("normal") English ...The King James Bible... "The language of men"... Many shades of meaning.

*E*nglish is the most widely used language in the history of the world. More people speak it than speak any other language—if we agree that the various forms of Chinese are, to all intents and purposes, separate languages. Millions of people also use English as a second language, as in India, where the differences among the dialects are so great that communities cannot communicate with one another in their native tongues. More of the world's printed matter is in English than in any other language, and there is more broadcasting in English than in all the other languages of the world combined.

English is a very rich language. Its literature is one of the great heritages of civilization. And its enormous vocabulary makes it infinitely flexible, capable of expressing the finest shades of meaning.

English is also a growing language. As the speech of the two nations that have led the world for the past hundred and fifty years in exploration, commerce, parliamentary government, war, and science, it has to keep pace with humanity's growing experience. The rate of growth seems to be accelerating rather than slowing down. In the twenty-seven years that elapsed between the publication of the *Second New International Dictionary* (1934) and the appearance of its successor, the *Third New International* (1961) the editors found it necessary to add 100,000 words and to drop 250,000 words that they felt had gone out of use.

Yet 1200 years ago, the rudiments of this great speech were confined to a few seafaring tribes inhabiting the coast of what is now part of Denmark and Holland. And even four hundred years ago, English was not regarded as one of the principal languages of Europe. Some authors who hoped for immortality translated their English writings into Latin, just to be on the safe side.

The original inhabitants of England were Celts. They spoke a language that survives in Gaelic, which is still spoken in parts of Ireland. Until recently, this was the living speech of hundreds of thousands of people in out-of-the-way places in Western England, Wales, Scotland and Ireland. Its persistence in the face of so many changes through so many centuries demonstrates the extraordinary tenacity and conservatism of speech.

For four hundred of these years—beginning with Julius Caesar in 55 B.C.—the Romans ruled England. They built great military roads, aqueducts, baths, amphitheaters and camps, but, except for the names of a few cities, made little impression on the language. Apparently the natives did not speak Latin, even through these long centuries, but stubbornly kept their Celtic.

In 410 A.D., Rome's Britannic legions were withdrawn. Soon afterwards bands of seafaring robbers, the Angles, Saxons, Jutes, and Norsemen, began to invade the country. At first they merely landed, robbed, and ran, but after a time they seized land, settled down, and brought boatloads of their kinsmen over to support them. By 800 A.D., the Celts—or at least their language— had been pushed back into the mountains of Wales and Scotland, and the chief speech of the land became a combination of the languages of the various Germanic tribes. It has been called Anglo-Saxon, but professional linguists today refer to it as Old English. This was a language much like its modern cousin, German. And it was a poetic language. The Anglo-Saxons did not think it was enough for a man to be a warrior. He had to be an orator as well. Above all other men, he was honored who, in their phrase, could "unlock the word hoard"—in other words, speak well.

Old English was a rhythmic language and highly alliterative. Its poetry employed complicated patterns of repeated initial consonants. Today, in such phrases as "busy as a bee," "cool as a cucumber," "might and main," and "rack and ruin," we still find pleasure in repeating an initial consonant.

Old English was almost entirely a spoken language. We have no evidence of its having been written down before the time of King Alfred, 900 A.D.

Yet though modern English is simply a developed form of this speech, barely forty percent of modern English words are of Old English origin. The rest are borrowed. For Old English was a spongelike language, taking for its own whatever useful words it found in other languages. The borrowings are primarily from French, Latin, and Greek, but there is scarcely a tongue that has not contributed something.

First of all, after the Saxon invaders had settled down and become peaceful folk, they were themselves invaded by the Danes and Vikings. These people were related by blood and language. The Saxons could understand their speech without much difficulty, so there was a natural mingling. Thus such common words as *husband*, *law*, *sky*, *ransack* and even the plural forms of our personal pronouns—*they*, *their*, *them*—are Scandinavian, not Saxon.

In other instances, however, both the Saxon *and* the Scandinavian forms were retained. *Shirt*, *screech*, *batch*, *watch* and *ditch* are Saxon and *skirt*, *shriek*, *bake*, *wake* and *dyke* are Scandinavian. And it will be noticed that slightly different meanings (*shirt*, *skirt*; *screech*, *shriek*; etc.) have become attached to different pronunciations.

In still other instances, the Scandinavian words drove out the Saxon word. *Take*, for example, is Scandinavian. The Saxon verb was *niman*, which seems very strange to us. We don't even recognize it when we use it in the word *nimble*. *Die* is Scandinavian. The Saxon was *steorfan* (German, *sterben*) which we keep in a specialized sense, *starve*, to die of hunger. In northern England, though, to this day *starve* keeps its old generalized meaning. On a raw winter day, someone may say that such-and-such a pinched, miserable-looking child is "fair starved with the cold."

Egg is Scandinavian, too. The Saxon word was *ei* (exactly like the modern German word) and was used in parts of England almost to Shakespeare's time. We know this from an incident that William Caxton, the first printer, relates. He tells the story in the preface to a translation of Virgil's *Aeneid* which he made from French in 1490. Speaking of the changeable nature of the English language, Caxton tells of a merchant who asked for eggs at a lonely farmhouse. The farmer's wife told him she didn't understand French, and since he didn't either, but was a true-born Englishman, he was annoyed. Then someone else at the farmhouse said maybe he meant *eiern*. (*Eiern* is the old plural of *ei*, as *oxen* is the plural of *ox*, and *children* of *child*). And, sure enough, she had plenty of those! Caxton mentions that the merchant's name was Sheffield. This may indicate that he came from the North, where the Scandinavian settlements had been stronger and their speech more deeply intermixed. In this little interchange we have a glimpse of how a language changes. For a merchant would then have been a very impressive figure to a farmwife, and this particular one would unquestionably have remembered all her days that important people call eggs *eggs*, not *eiern*. She most likely called them *eggs* herself thereafter, and corrected her more ignorant neighbors.

After the Scandinavian and Danish raids, England was not invaded again until the eleventh century. In 1066 William of Normandy conquered England. It was a small affair by modern military standards, and was accomplished with relatively little bloodshed. But it had such far-reaching effects, historically and linguistically, that scholars usually list it among the most significant events in history.

At first it did not seem to make much difference to the language. The Normans were the descendants of Vikings who invaded France several generations before (*Norman* is a shortening of *Nor(se)man*). But their speech was a form of French which, in turn, is a development of Latin. As is common with a dominant group after such an invasion (like the British in India, the French in Indochina, the Spanish in the Americas), the conquerors went right on speaking their own language and the conquered went on speaking their language, Old English. The conquerors, as conquerors do, lived in ease and luxury. They left the hard work for the conquered. How do we know this? The language shows it. Thus the names for certain domesticated animals while they are alive and hence need caring for are Old English: *cow*, *sheep*, *swine*. But when they are ready to be eaten, they are Norman French: *beef*, *mutton*, *pork*. Plain words for plain fare were Old English: *meal*, *food*, *eat*. But *feast*, *banquet*, and *dine* are French. So *work* is Old English, but *leisure* is French.

The real effect of the Conquest on England—far more important than any amount of word borrowing—was that it drew England into the culture of Western Europe. Up to that time, England had been isolated.

In time, by means of direct borrowing and indirect associating, thousands of French words were added to the common stock of English, but the two languages never completely blended. Since the King and his court spoke French, as did all the higher clergymen, the native language was soon driven out of polite and educated use. Only the peasants (the *churls*) used it. Since nobody of any position or authority cared in the least *how* they used it, the tendency to drop its endings was greatly accelerated. And the process is continuing right to our day. For instance, a newspaper will print CUBA CRISIS instead of CUBAN CRISIS.

But for all its social advantages, Norman French did not replace Old English. Two hundred years after the Conquest, English ("Angle-ish") conquered its conquerors. It emerged once again as the language of all the people, of the learned and powerful as well as of the ignorant and lowly. Scholars refer to this later stage of development as Middle English. But it was much changed. Unless one has had special training, Old English is a completely foreign language. But anyone who can read modern English can stumble through the Middle English of Chaucer and make a fairly good guess at the meaning most of the time. Indeed, with twenty minutes' explanation of the language and a special list of not more than 200 words, any reader today could make out 90 percent of Chaucer.

Part of the difficulty that we have with Chaucer today is not that his English is so strange, but that his *French* is so strange. By the end of the fourteenth century, educated Englishmen had adopted so much of European culture that they didn't know quite what language they *ought* to speak. Langland was still writing English on the pattern of Old English verse. Chaucer probably spoke French as naturally as he spoke Middle English, but he wrote in Middle English with many French borrowings. John Gower wrote a long work in each of three languages—Middle English, French, and Latin.

Even those who spoke English did not necessarily speak alike. There were many widely different dialects. But the head-quarters of both church and state were in London. This meant that people of learning, lawyers, courtiers, and captains had their fixed headquarters in London. And since London was also the commercial capital and commerce was expanding, the London dialect came to be *the* dialect. In time, it was accepted as the standard, the "normal" way of speaking and writing.

The Tudor period (1485-1603) ushered in the modern world. An age of commerce and exploration replaced the age of feudalism. The Renaissance, or revival of classical learning, fired people's minds with a new and wonderful excitement. The invention of printing spread knowledge to the masses. The theater made great poetry as common a diversion as westerns or comic strips are today. The Bible was translated into the language people spoke and could understand. For a hundred years it progressed through numerous versions to flower, in 1611, in the King James Version, one of the greatest single books in any language. Its wording, by the way, was extremely conservative. Everyone felt that the word of God should not be lightly tampered with. And this did much to uphold the dominance of early English words in our speech.

Elsewhere, English, still uncertain of itself, went off into verbal pinwheels and skyrockets which, even today, take our breath away. Many of the great speeches in Shakespeare's plays are dramatically inappropriate and, under the circumstances represented on the stage, more than improbable. But that didn't matter in the least. The Elizabethan audience accepted poetic passages, in fact demanded them. They wanted to hear rolling words. The whole age was drunk on words.

And this was the speech which the first colonists brought to America. In many ways, American English retains characteristics of Elizabethan English. We hear its plain accent in many rural places still. It shows in our vocabulary and in our grammar and, above all, in the vitality of our way of speaking—slangy, hasty, playful, often insulting.

The Renaissance brought a flood of Latin words into English. It has been estimated that English has absorbed a full fourth of the entire Latin vocabulary—though much came by way of French and not directly. Among the learned, English took on so many Latin forms that, as one writer said at the time, a person almost had to learn Latin to understand English. Some of the Latinized words seem mighty strange today: *basiate* (kiss), *deblaterate* (babble), *exilitie* (slenderness) and others.

The Elizabethan age and the century that followed it were periods of great excitement and excess—of too much vitality, too much learning, too much passion, too much indulging in the sound of words. And, as was inevitable, this period of excess was followed in the eighteenth century by a period of strict formality and restraint. It distrusted all excess, all passion even, and gradually strangled itself in rules and regulations—both for art and life.

Then, at the beginning of the nineteenth century, the poet William Wordsworth led a counter-revolution against all this formality. In a famous manifesto, he called on poets to write "in the language of men." Despite the conservatism that continued through the Victorian period, today the gap between written and spoken English is narrower than at any time since the Elizabethan age.

Many people, especially older people educated in the Victorian tradition, dislike this narrowing. They never stop crying about the "degeneration" of the language. But the process continues, whether it is degeneration or progress. We must accept it as one of the characteristics of contemporary English. Merriam-Webster's *Third International* dropped the classification *colloquial* (conversational) because its editors believe there is no longer a clear distinction between colloquial and standard English. And the *London Times Literary Supplement*, in a special issue (August 10, 1962) devoted to the language, stated that "standard English no longer exists."

Whether it does or not, whatever English has become as it has spread around the globe, there is no doubt that it has acquired an enormous vocabulary by the simple process of borrowing. If we count different words, three fifths of English is borrowed from other languages. If we count the words used, two thirds of the words we speak are native. That is, English reflects its traditional Germanic origins, but is enriched and embroidered over with other languages.

We have already commented on the Scandinavian borrowings. Latin borrowings began with words connected with the Church and its services (*candle*, *deacon*, *priest*). They entered the language through special usage—grammatical terms, musical terms, scientific terms, and so on. But most of the Latin in English came indirectly, through French. French has, indeed, been a sort of funnel through which Latin has flowed into English ever since the Norman Conquest. Goods and fashions, armor, clothing, cooking—all came into England from the Continent by way of France, and brought their own vocabularies along with them.

There have been waves of such borrowing. English words which have been borrowed at different times from French show the changes that took place in *French* words. Thus when a *ch* in an English word that was originally French is pronounced as in *change* or *chant*, it was borrowed many years ago. We know because that's the way *ch* used to be pronounced in French. When a *ch* is pronounced *sh* as in *champagne*, we know the borrowing is more recent, because this is the more recent French pronunciation. Sometimes we borrowed the same word twice. Meanwhile, it may have acquired a new, specialized meaning in French. So *chief*, an old borrowing, has the old pronunciation, while *chef* (which means chief cook), more recent, has the newer pronunciation.

For more than two centuries the Normans dominated the law courts, and our law terminology is rich in French additions (*mortgage*, *lease*, *perjury*, *embezzle*, *brief*).

Other French borrowings are *caprice*, *foible*, *intrigue*, *critic*, and so on. (The borrrowing isn't wholly one way, of course.

French has borrowed from English. Almost all terms for sports in French are English. And sometimes English borrows back a word which French has taken in the first place. Thus the French borrowed the English *riding coat*, which in their pronunciation and spelling became *redingote*. English reborrowed it as a name for a special kind of full-length coat.)

English has borrowed more from French than from any other language. But this was merely an accident of geography and history. France was the nearest country and England was continually at war with her. But the borrowing tendency in the language is completely impartial and will pick up any word anywhere.

A list of a few borrowings will bring home the wide range of this selecting. *Dim*, *clan*, *whiskey*, and *slogan* are Celtic. *Embargo*, *cargo*, *sherry*, *comrade*, *alligator*, and *calaboose* are Spanish. From the Dutch, we have *yacht*, *deck*, *easel*, *sketch*, *landscape*, *cruise*, and *isinglass*. *Julep*, *bazaar*, and *caravan* are Persian. We borrowed *sugar*, *syrup*, *harem*, and *cipher* from Arabic. *Shampoo*, *juggernaut*, and *bungalow* are from India. *Chocolate* and *tomato* are Aztec, by way of Spanish. *Steppe*, *icon*, *knout*, and *samovar* are Russian.

Borrowing not only affords us many words but many shades of meaning among the words we may choose from. The language is infinitely rich. No one has ever mastered all of its possibilities, or ever will. Though hundreds of millions speak it, every one can find full expression for his or her own individuality in it.

5

Vocabulary Building

*Adapting words...New words...Accidental words...
Invented words...Words from proper names...Joined
words...Shortened words...Blending...Affixes...
Common suffixes.*

*I*n borrowing so freely, the English language did just what we
do as individuals to increase our personal vocabularies. When
we see something strange or experience something new,
either we take the name for it that someone else—whether a
foreigner or not—is using or, on the basis of some real or fancied
resemblance, we take an old word and apply it in a new situation.
This gives it a new meaning and us a new word.

Kangaroo is an example. Captain Cook first saw a kangaroo
during his exploration of the South Pacific (1768-1771). No
European language had a name for this animal, much less an
idea of it. It was a very strange and exciting thing. Therefore, it
had to be talked about at once and that meant it had to have a
name. There is a story that when Cook asked a native what the
animal was, the native, in his own tongue, said "I don't understand you." Since that statement sounded something like "Kangaroo," Cook mistook it for the creature's name and forthwith
called it that.

Though Cook does not tell the story himself, it is a very old
story and may very well be true. Nobody has ever found any word
in any known Australian native language that describes the beast
and sounds like *kangaroo*. But then, according to the story, that
wasn't what the native really said anyway. And the story certainly
illustrates a common event in conversation. A asks B a question
which B doesn't understand. B gives A an answer which A doesn't
understand, but thinks he or she does. Both go along under the
impression that they have communicated with each other.

At any rate, *kangaroo* is now the animal's name in English.
A word which had never appeared in any European tongue before

31

the latter part of the seventeenth century, and has never been traced to any Australian dialect, is now as fixed in the language as if it could be traced back to Latin. It's accepted as much as *wolf* or *rabbit* or any other name for an animal.

Several generations after the Cook expedition, during the California gold rush, the word suddenly acquired a new meaning. Vigilante courts which passed hasty judgment on various offenders or victims were called "kangaroo courts." Again, no one knows quite why. Some believe that it was due to their organization by Australian miners who had come to California by way of Hawaii. Others think it may have reflected the fact that many of those hailed before such courts had been guilty of claim-jumping. But, whatever its basis, it, too, has passed into the language.

In addition to borrowing and adapting, the language has other ways of increasing its store of words. For instance, instead of borrowing a foreign word, it may make up the idea expressed in a foreign word out of its own elements. This was a strong tendency in Old English at first, when it seemed to resist borrowing. Thus, instead of just accepting the Latin *archangelus* (archangel), Old English substituted *heāhboda* (high-abider, high-dweller). Instead of adopting *commiserate*, it made up *efensārgian* (equal-sorrowing).

Most of these creations were lost, but a few stuck, such as *godspell* for *evangelium* and *withstand* for *oppose*. In the nineteenth century, there was a strong effort to revive this principle rather than to borrow. This effort produced such oddities as *pushwainling* for *perambulator* (though the American *baby carriage* was more natural and more lasting) and at least one or two words that became standard: *handbook* for *manual* and *foreword* for *preface*.

This tendency is still strong in German, but it has lost its force in English. Maybe the churls got so used to hearing Norman French as well as Old English that they lost all feeling for the correctness of one language over another. They just took whatever word was handy.

Or they made up wholly new words, or reshaped old words, even when they didn't understand them. Or they ran simple words together to meet a complex idea. They might take a root, and by adding suffixes and prefixes, extend the basic meaning. Or they did any one of several other things which we say are "natural" to the language, and which we go right on doing every day, and will continue to do as long as we and the language are alive.

These things are worth examining because an awareness of

the way words are formed enables us to extend our own vocabularies and to grasp the meaning of thousands of additional words.

There is a great deal we don't know about our language and especially about many individual words in it. The only way we can know anything about a word's former use, of course, is by finding it written down, used in a way that either makes its meaning clear or shows that the meaning we now give it doesn't fit the former use. For instance, we read in the *Book of Jeremiah* in the Bible that of two baskets of figs, "One basket has very good figs, even like the figs that are first ripe; and the other basket had very naughty figs, which could not be eaten, they were so bad." Plainly the meaning of *naughty* has changed.

And since we do not find all words in such illuminating contexts, we may only know that we are ignorant about many of them. They were either there at the beginning of the written record (like *quiver*—for men had quivers probably long before they had writing) or they just suddenly appeared with very much their modern meanings. Thus Chaucer says that among his pilgrims going to Canterbury in the late fourteenth century was a haberdasher. And so, like the kangaroo, there was suddenly a haberdasher. He's with us yet, doing business at the old stand. But what the origin of the word *haberdasher* may be, no one knows for certain.

In the same manner, *dog* and *pig* appeared in the twelfth century. And a hundred years later, *big, bad, cut,* and *fog.* And later still, *jump, brave, fun, flute,* and *zinc.* And in our own time, *bogus, sundae, jitney, jalopy, moxie, charleyhorse, boondocks,* and hundreds of others. By "appeared," we mean "appeared in writing or print." The word may have been in daily use for a thousand years, but unless it was set down (or in recent times, recorded) we would not know it had existed.

Some words are just accidents. *Helpmeet, scapegoat, derring-do* and several other words were, originally, misunderstandings (something like the common use of *gorilla* for *guerrilla*). Hundreds of others owe their form or pronunciation to confusion or ignorance. The *s,* for instance, doesn't belong in *island,* or the *c* in *scythe,* or the *l* in *could,* or the *r* in *trousers.* That is, it was not there historically. It was inserted through some misunderstanding in the course of the word's development. Sometimes a sound jumps around inside a word and so in time affects the spelling. *Wasp* was once *wops* and *ask*—as some children still pronounce it—*axe.*

Thousands of words have been deliberately invented and hundreds of these have passed into general use. We know that the

Dutch chemist Van Helmont invented the word *gas* in 1652 and that the German physicist Karl von Reichenbach made up the word *paraffin* (1830). Earlier Sir Isaac Newton had coined *centrifugal* and *centripetal* and Robert Boyle made up *pendulum* and *intensity*. To Edmund Burke, the great statesman, we owe *diplomacy, electioneering, federalism,* and *municipality*. And Coleridge, the author of *The Rime of the Ancient Mariner*, gave us *pessimism, intensify,* and *phenomenal*. Edmund Spenser coined *blatant*; Milton, *pandemonium*; and Thomas Carlyle, *self-help*.

Anyone is free to make up any word he or she wants to. One may merely imitate a sound connected with a thing or an action, as in *thump, rattle, bang, fizz, whistle*. Or may just put letters together. During our lifetime, Gelett Burgess coined *blurb* to describe the extravagant praise a publisher puts on a book's jacket. But except for the fun of doing it, it's likely to be a wasted effort. A word has to gain public acceptance before it can be thought of as a part of the language.

Many words are derived from proper names, as *sandwich* from John Montagu, the Earl of Sandwich. Montagu was an inveterate gambler who would not leave the gaming table to eat, but had meat brought to him between slices of bread. *Pompadour* comes from the Marquise of Pompadour (d. 1764), Louis XV's mistress, who wore her hair in the fashion her name now describes. *Guy* is derived from Guy Fawkes, *pasteurize* from Louis Pasteur. And so on. But, of course, such words can't be invented. The name of some person just happens to become associated with a thing.

Many words, in the form we now have them, are due to twisting a strange word to make it fit an assumed meaning. *Crayfish*, for example, is from the French *écrevisse*. But since the creature lives in water, someone decided the second element must be the English *-fish*. In many rural places, the process has been carried still further to *crawfish*, the first element having been changed to correspond to *crawl*. *Belfry* originally was *bergfrid*, a watchtower. It had nothing to do with bells.

The *hope* of *forlorn hope* is not our word for favorable expectation, but is the Dutch *hoop*, "heap." *Verloren hoop* was a Dutch military term referring to what we now call "suicide squads." A *wiseacre* was a *wijsseggher* or wise-sayer. *Trade winds* may assist trade, but they were so called because they move in a set or trodden course. *Penthouse* once had no connection with the word *house*. It was a *pentis* or *pentus*, something appended to a building or, as we now describe it, a lean-to. Such words, of course, are rarely coined deliberately. They come into being by chance and glide unnoticed into common acceptance.

But there are thousands of words that were obviously shaped by deliberate intent. Among them are those words that were formed by the joining of other words. This is one of the strongest formative processes in English. Almost any part of speech can be joined to another part of speech if it produces the word wanted. We join nouns with nouns (*railroad, head cold, sweat shop*); or nouns with adjectives (*ice-cold, heartsick, airtight*); or adjectives with nouns (*hot house*); or adverbs with nouns (*afterthought*); or verbs with adverbs (*kickoff, runaway*); or nouns with verbs (*sideswipe*); or verbs with nouns (*playboy*). Sometimes we stick three words together and get such results as *notwithstanding, nevertheless, mother-in-law,* and *hand-me-downs.*

The Elizabethans loved this sort of compounding. Many of their creations have fallen into disuse (*wantwit, ticklebrain, tosspot, sneakjack*) but others became permanent (*killjoy, scarecrow, hangdog, slipshod*). And we Americans share the pleasure of such creations (*bellhop, jailbird, bootlegger, skinflint*).

Once the compound is in general use, we become unaware of its elements. We don't think of a *skyscaper* as scraping the sky. All idea of folding has faded from *implicate,* and we are a little startled to discover that *solution* is hidden in *absolute.*

As we form some words by adding, we form others by taking away, or shortening. Most people now say *phone* though they would probably write *telephone* in any formal document. But they would both say and write *bus* not *omnibus.* So *wig, still, sport, spite,* and *fence* are now fully legitimate in themselves; we do not think of them as clippings of *periwig, distillery, disport, despite,* and *defense* (earlier, *defence*). And we accept *mob* for *mobile vulgus, cab* for *cabriolet, gas* for *gasoline,* and *canter* for *Canterbury gallop.* We often hear *perk* used in place of *percolate,* but it is informal. *Gym* is universal in schools and colleges, but those who use it would probably write *gymnasium* in a report or statement.

Back formation is another way of forming words in English. That is, a word will be formed from one that looks like its derivative. Thus the verb *typewrite* was formed from the noun *typewriter,* and *diagnose* from *diagnosis. Enthuse* is in the process of being formed from *enthusiastic,* but it isn't fully accepted yet, and many people are indignant whenever they hear or see it. The same is true of *emote* and *emotion.* Yet they accept *to jell, to peddle, to beg, to preach, to grovel, to donate, to edit,* and scores of other words formed in exactly the same manner. Not that they accept some and reject others on principle. They probably just don't know that these common, standard words are, linguistically, on a par with *to enthuse* and *to emote*.

Another way in which words are formed is by blending. Two words are telescoped to form a word that conveys their combined meanings. Lewis Carroll played with this feature of language in *Through the Looking Glass* where he has Humpty-Dumpty explain to Alice some of the odd words used in the poem "Jabberwocky." *Slithy,* for instance, meant *slimy* and *lithe.* *Mimsy* is *miserable* and *flimsy.* And to *chortle* is to *chuckle* and *snort* at the same time.

In the same manner, we have combined *clap* and *crash* to get *clash,* *gleam* and *shimmer* to get *glimmer,* *flame* and *glare* to get *flare,* *growl* and *rumble* to get *grumble,* *slip* and *glide* to form *slide,* and so on.

This process is very active in American English today and has given us *brunch* (breakfast and lunch), *motel* (motor and hotel), *contrail* (condensation trail), and hundreds of others. It's very fashionable in slick journalism. Many such creations add sparkle to one or two magazine issues and then disappear (*globaloney, infanticipating, urbanality*). But their short life in no way detracts from their effectiveness when they are used. There's no reason why every word should last forever.

The most active process of all in the formation of English words is the use of affixes. Affixes are elements attached to the stem or base of a word, elements that are not used by themselves, but that add a definite meaning to the word they become a part of. When they are attached before the stem, they are called prefixes; when they are attached after the stem, they are called suffixes. And anybody at all adventurous in speech will make them up by the dozen every day.

The prefix *un-* illustrates the use and complexity of the affix in English. It can make an adjective mean its opposite, as when it changes *happy* to *unhappy* and *clear* to *unclear.* And it can do the same for a verb, as when it changes *tie* to *untie* and *do* to *undo.* But where the verb is already negative, *un-* seems to have no effect on the meaning. *Ravel* means the same as *unravel*; *loose* means the same as *unloose.*

There is no real difference beween the two negative prefixes *un-* and *in-,* though a tendency is developing to use *in-* when the base is a borrowed word. Thus we say *unthinkable* and *unlikable* (*think* and *like* being English words), but *inexorable* and *incred-*

ible (-*exorable* and *credible* being Latin derivatives). Earlier English had *unglorious, unpossible*, and *unexperienced*, but these have been changed to *inglorious, impossible*, and *inexperienced*.

But the change is far from universal (we still have *undesirable, unprogressive* and others) and probably never will be. Very few people know or care whether a word is native or foreign. And the matter is further complicated by the fact that *in-* has two, almost opposite, meanings. One meaning of *in-* is negative, as *indiscreet, insincere*. But the other serves as an intensive, emphasizing rather than changing the original meaning, as *inflammable*. In fact, the confusion of whether inflammable means "capable of burning" or "not capable of burning" has led some government agencies to insist on marking burnable goods *flammable* for clarity. Affixes are so important in English that sometimes the word formed with the prefix or suffix completely overshadows the basic word. Then we lose the old word. Thus we have *uncouth* but have forgotten *couth*. We have *ungainly* and *insipid* but have forgotten *gainly* and *sipid*. Everybody uses *ruthless* and *reckless*, but it is rarely that one finds the old *ruth* and *reck*.

There are styles in affixes. *Anti-* (against) and *extra-* (outside of, in addition to) are very popular now. So are *un-* in some ultra-smart contexts (*unwork, unmusic*). And how would we get through a single day without *-ize* (*miniaturize, finalize*).

In all Indo-European languages (of which English is one), suffixes play a much greater role in word formation than do prefixes. We change endings rather than beginnings of words. Suffixing does more to form the language and increase the scope of its vocabulary than all other methods combined.

Adding a suffix is a far subtler business than the ordinary speaker of the language has any idea of. One does it without realizing it. Thus one of the commonest suffixes in English consists of changing a final consonant, though often very slightly, to indicate a change in function. Mention this to the ordinary speaker of the language, and he or she would probably be unable to recall a single instance. Yet once it is pointed out, we can see that the noun *house* ends in a slightly different sound than does the verb *to house*, like the noun *wreath* and the verb *to wreathe* and *breath* and *to breathe*. In these and many other words, we voice the final consonant to mark a change in function.

Most suffixes are more obvious. We probably do not learn them as suffixes, however. We probably learn each separate word and from the "feel" of some particular word in a particular context, extend its suffix to another stem.

Among the commonest of our suffixes:

-ish means belonging to or having the characteristics of (*boyish*) or addicted to (*bookish*). But it is frequently uncomplimentary, suggesting an unsuitable resemblance (*childish, mannish*).

-ist often carries a feeling of contempt (*nudist, faddist, militarist, defeatist*). Sometimes the contempt is forgotten and the word becomes a term of respect. *Methodist* is a striking example. And *chemist* may once have been unflattering.

-ly when it equals "having the nature of" is favorable in connotations (*manly, kingly, motherly*).

-like, in the formation of adjectives, is usually complimentary (*childlike, godlike*), but in the formation of adverbs, it can be slightly uncomplimentary: "Gorillalike, he thumped his chest."

The suffixes *-er*, *-or* indicate an agent of action (a *fighter*, one who fights; a *doer*, one who does; a *vendor*, one who sells, or vends). A distinction seems to be in the process of being established whereby *-or* shall mark a trade, profession, or skill and *-er* shall mark merely the doer of an action. Thus one who goes regularly to sea is a *sailor*, but one who on one occasion only sails a boat would be the *sailer* of the boat. A bookie might be a *bettor*, but the amateur victim would be a *better*. But this distinction is far from established, and one who gives advice may still be either an *advisor* or an *adviser*.

-ster is a variant of *-er*. It now differs from *-er* in conveying reproach (*gangster, punster, jokester*). This may be due to the assumption that it is a feminine suffix (*spinster*), though it isn't. It is retained in its older, nonreproachful meaning in many personal names (*Baxter, Webster, Dempster*).

One of the commonest of our suffixes *-ship* (related far off, it may be, to *shape*) is used to denote a state or condition of being (*hardship*), a dignity or rank (*lordship, worship*), a state of life, an occupation or behavior (*courtship, penmanship, brinkmanship*), or to indicate a sense of collectiveness (*township*). *Seamanship*, by the way, is related to *-ship*, not to *ship*.

-ling indicates smallness (*duckling*) and, possibly because small things are frequently despised, contempt (*princeling*).

Two of the most active suffixes today are *-ee* and *-wise*. *-ee* is used increasingly to indicate someone to whom something has been done (*divorcee, payee, enlistee*), and we overwork it. In newspapers, we always find such words as *honoree* (one honored) and *retiree* (one who has been retired).

-wise is often used a great deal to mean "in respect to" or "considered from the viewpoint of." We are told that "dollarwise" this or that is not a bargain, or that "coursewise" the curriculum is unbalanced, or that "camerawise" the movie was excellent. Linguistically the suffix is warranted in many of these instances, but it is overworked to the point of annoyance. As an amusing article in *Harper's Magazine* noted: "I Am Fedwise Up."

As an extreme example of the way in which a word can develop in English through the use of affixes, consider the old spelling-bee jawbreaker: *antidisestablishmentarianism*. There actually is such a word and it has been used, though, plainly, if you took to throwing it around, the conversation would simply cave in.

Its central idea is *-stable-*, from the Latin *stare*, to stand. *-ish* is a suffix forming simple verbs; hence *establish* (the prefatory *e-* came from the French pronunciation) meant "the act of making stable." To this was added *-ment*, a noun suffix denoting an act or state resulting from (as *refreshment* is the act of being refreshed or the state resulting from being refreshed). So *establishment* is the state of being established, or by logical extension, something established. In the particular sense attached to this particular word, it was the Church of England which was or was not to be established as the state Church.

The next element, *-arian*, can mean one who believes in something as a sort of doctrine. To illustrate, a *vegetarian* differs from a mere eater of vegetables. A vegetable-eater may eat vegetables only because he can't get anything else, or because they are cheap, or because he eats them as leftovers. But a vegetarian eats vegetables because he or she believes one should.

Now the establishment of the Church of England as *the* state Church was fiercely contested. In fact, it was one of the major causes of a civil war. There were those who believed in it with sufficient religious fervor to warrant being called *establishmentarians*.

-ism, which is now a very popular suffix, means a doctrine or theory. So that *establishmentarianism* meant the theory or doctrine of the establishmentarians. But there were those who held an opposing doctrine, that the church should be *dis*established. And their doctrine was *disestablishmentarianism*. But when they agitated in Parliament to have their doctrine made into law, there were many who opposed them and were firmly against

(*anti-*) their teaching. These were the antidisestablishmentarians and their doctrine was *antidisestablishmentarianism!*

Thus three prefixes and four suffixes were added to the stem -*stable*-, each addition carrying the word into a new meaning. To thread one's way through the maze of its changing meanings is an exercise in affixation. But it is worth it if it brings home to us the infinite capacity of English to develop new words and new shades of meaning from an already enormous list.

6

The Dictionary

What a good dictionary offers... Using a dictionary... New meanings of old words... Dr. Johnson, Noah Webster, the Oxford English Dictionary... Change in language... Custom makes correctness... The thesaurus.

Dictionaries come in all sizes, from small paperbacks which cost very little, to the huge thirteen-volume *Oxford English Dictionary* which costs as much as a fairly expensive television set.

The little volumes are tempting in their handy size and low cost, but some of them are inadequate. The great dictionaries are awkward to handle and are not intended for the beginner. However, if you do not have at least one good desk dictionary (they cost around fifteen dollars), it is hard to believe that you have a serious interest in improving your command of words.

A good dictionary offers American spellings, division into syllables, and pronunciation. It will tell you what part of speech the word is. It will give a brief statement of the origin (derivation) of the word. Under numbered headings, it will give the word's various meanings, including specialized meanings. Where seeing the word's use in a phrase or sentence will make a certain meaning clearer, it will also give examples. Illustrations may also be given.

Any good dictionary has a selective treatment of synonyms and antonyms; that is, words which mean the same as the word being discussed and words which mean the opposite. Where the similar meanings are identical and the opposed meanings obvious, the dictionary may merely list them. But where there are fine shades of difference, it will discuss them to make the distinctions clear.

A dictionary also identifies scientific, technological, geographical, and biographical items insofar as they make a word clear.

Every dictionary is self-explanatory. The symbols and markings may be a little puzzling at first, but since a dictionary could not give you one tenth of the information it does without them, they are worth mastering. It is most important to read the introductory material at the front of the dictionary in order to get the full benefit of your dictionary. This includes a statement of the principles on which the dictionary is based, gives the order of meanings (from old to new, or from new to old), explains the meaning of the terms used, and tells you where and how to look for further related information. All of this is essential. And it isn't nearly so difficult as the instructions for assembling a household gadget or a Christmas toy.

There is a great deal of information packed in the short phrases, abbreviations, symbols, and markings. We must admit rather regretfully that not one user out of a hundred gets all that a good dictionary offers him. Either he or she is unwilling to go to the slight trouble necessary to understand the abbreviations and symbols, or he or she just doesn't know how to go about understanding them.

Let us look at the word *vocabulary* in *The Random House College Dictionary*—one of the very best of the desk dictionaries—and see what it tells us. The entry reads:

vo·cab·u·lar·y (vō kab'yə ler'ē), *n.*, *pl.* **-lar·ies.** **1.**the stock of words used by or known to a particular person or group of persons. **2.** a list or collection of the words or phrases of a language, technical field, etc., usually arranged in alphabetical order and defined. **3.** the words of a language. **4.** any more or less specific group of forms characteristic of an artist, a style of art, architecture, or the like. [› ML *vocābulāri(um)*, neut. of *vocābulārius* of words. See VOCABLE, -ARY]

At the outset the dots between certain of the letters divide the word into syllables. This might seem to be obvious, but it isn't. Information about syllables is important to have because it is related to the word's pronunciation. It will help indicate its origin and development. Syllabification is also a guide to the correct division of the word. In writing it, you may have to divide it at the end of one line and carry a part of it over into the next line.

Then, in parentheses, we are given the pronunciation. We learn that the *o* is pronounced as in *over*; the first *a* as in *act*; that the *u* is scarcely pronounced at all (that is, that it is given the faint *uh* sound that *a* has in the word *alone*); that the second *a* is not pronounced like an *a* at all but like the *e* in *ebb*; and that the final letter, the *y*, is pronounced like the *e* in *equal*. The heavy accent mark following *kab* (the ' sign) tells us that we put the chief stress on that syllable. A lighter mark of the same kind tells us that a lesser, secondary, stress falls on the syllable *ler*.

But, you may ask, how does the user of the dictionary know this? The answer is simple: it is repeated at the foot of every other page. When you open the dictionary, you will find at the foot of every right-hand page examples of the various vowel sounds in words whose pronunciation is quite familiar to you. This information is repeated more than 750 times throughout the dictionary.

After the pronunciation, the dictionary tells us that *vocabulary* is a noun (*"n."*) and that its plural is *(vocabu)laries*.

After that come the various meanings. The first definition tells us that *vocabulary* can be applied to the stock of words used by a group of people (a nation, a profession, a teen-age gang, any group whatever), or the stock of words used by a single person (as "The boy's vocabulary was limited," "The editor's vocabulary was large").

The second definition tells us that *vocabulary* also applies to a list of words, whether an entire language, a particular book, a special branch of science, or some individual author. It adds the information that such a list is usually in alphabetical order and carries definitions. (Note that "usually" implies that such order or the giving of definitions does not always occur, nor does it have to.)

In the third definition the dictionary tells us that *vocabulary* can mean the words of a language. This might seem repetitious. But if we consider it carefully, we will see that it says something slightly different from anything that has been said in definitions 1 and 2. This should heighten the reader's awareness of slight differences while reminding him of the immense amount of thought that has gone into the dictionary's definitions. It should convince him of how important it is to consult one.

The fourth definition shows us that *vocabulary* can be used figuratively to describe the forms characteristic of an artist or style of art.

If, by chance, you found that the man sitting next to you on a train or plane was the editor of a great dictionary, you would probably be excited. This would be a rare opportunity to talk about the meaning and use of certain words that had long puzzled you. But he would be the first to insist that he could not know one thousandth of what was in his dictionary, even of the entries that he might have written himself.

By using the dictionary, checked for accuracy and continually revised, you have at your immediate command the lifetime effort of hundreds of editors at their deliberate best. It is very important that a dictionary be up-to-date. Any editor of a good dictionary would insist that his dictionary does *not* tell you the "correct" usage. It records what people say and write. This seems to disturb many people, despite lexicographers' efforts to make it clear. It is not that they wish to get rid of the responsibility, as is sometimes charged, but because the nature of language makes it all a dictionary can do.

Take, for example, so seemingly simple a matter as defining the word *door*. Surely, one would think, there are things called doors and they can be defined. And so they can. But only in terms of what those who speak the language mean by *door*. And that isn't simple. Even after you have distinguished among trap doors, cellar doors, tent flaps, and the massive, electrically controlled slabs that close plane hangars, you have a number of closing devices that might be considered gates or screens just as well as doors. And new ways of building, new materials, new inventions to close off indoor spaces have all added to the possible meanings of *door*.

International discovered *door* had many meanings in 1961 that it didn't have in 1934 when they issued the *Second International*. And as conscientious editors they had to record all of them.

Therefore we must not only buy a dictionary, but buy a new one at least every ten years.

Even then, of course, it won't be completely up-to-date. It takes many years to put together or even revise a dictionary. There is always a slight lag between what a dictionary records and how its users speak.

Take the word *silo*. Until very recently, the sole meaning of the word to Americans was a tall cylindrical structure seen on farms and used to store fodder. But we are constantly reading about a different kind of silo in our newspapers. (The old silos are as useful as ever but not very newsworthy). The new silo is an underground structure used for storing guided missiles in readiness for firing. Dictionaries a few decades ago did not give this meaning. It didn't exist then. But it wasn't the dictionaries that gave it meaning. They merely record that this new meaning has come into general use.

Or consider the common phrase "the coast." To most Americans, this means a seashore or the land near it, a littoral. But in the American theatrical, television, advertising, and public-relations world, and throughout most of the city of New York, it means a specific coast: California, especially Los Angeles. Even the conservative *New York Times* uses it, without any indication that it is informal English. And since the *Times*, more than any other publication, influences the standard of what is standard English, this meaning will have to be recorded. As yet, however, it is still considered informal.

Dictionaries have not always had the function they do today. It has evolved through centuries of experience. The first lists that undertook to explain the meanings of words dealt with foreign languages and were usually in Latin. They were called glosses or glossaries and were for the use of scribes in monasteries. Some of those used in England go back to the seventh century.

As the language began to develop national characteristics, Latin explanations gave way to English. By the middle of the fifteenth century, dictionaries which gave English equivalents of Latin words began to appear. The first real English dictionary was Robert Cawdrey's *Table Alphabeticall*, which was published in 1604. But it made no pretense of explaining every word. It dealt only with what were thought to be hard words—some 3,000 in all. The first that thought it worthwhile to attempt to explain the origins of words was Thomas Blount's *Glossographia* in 1656.

By the eighteenth century, there were a number of dictionaries, many with special new features. Kersey's *New English Dictionary* (1702), for instance, emphasized words most commonly used.

Even then people were aware that the language was changing. And then, as now, most people felt that something should be done to stop it. So the London publishers banded together and hired Samuel Johnson (he had not yet become the famous *Dr.* Johnson) to compile a dictionary that would "fix" the language and put an end to what they looked on as "corruption" and "decay."

Johnson had no special qualifications as a lexicographer, but he knew a tremendous amount of Latin and a great deal of English. He had a mind like a rock crusher and a remarkable talent for definition. He was intelligent, honest, capable of learning from experience, and he was willing to reverse himself when he found out that he had been wrong.

The dictionary, which appeared in 1755, turned out to be quite different in some respects from what had been expected. When undertaking the task, Johnson had announced that he would "fix" the pronunciation of English, "preserve the purity" of its idiom, brand "impure" words with a "note of infamy" and, in general, put a stop to the degenerative process which bothered Lord Chesterfield and some other literary people.

But in working on the dictionary, Johnson discovered that this neither could nor should be done. He decided that language is neither "permanent nor stable" but is "produced by necessity and enlarged by accident." According to Johnson, there are no guides in it except "experience and analogy" and it was foolish to attempt to arrest the changes of a living speech. One might as well "lash the wind," he said in a famous preface, as to try to "enchain syllables." The causes of change in language are as much beyond human control as the movements of the stars or the inrushing of the tide.

Finding that he could not lay down rules, Johnson gave actual examples to show current meaning and form. And by offering illustrative quotations as his final authority, he established what is now a basic principle in linguistics—that language is solely what usage makes it and that custom, in the long run, is the ultimate and only court of appeal as to what is "correct" in speech.

Since the publication of Johnson's dictionary, this principle has shaped every dictionary, not because of the weight of his great name but simply because everybody who has worked with words has found out that Johnson was right. There isn't any choice. At the appearance of each new revision of the leading dictionaries, there is invariably an outcry from many who feel that the acceptance of change marks acceptance of "corruption" and "decay." But these very people—many of whom are editors and professional writers—couldn't sell a line they wrote if they believed what they said. They would have to write in the language of a previous generation. And, as a matter of fact, the revision of the dictionaries is necessitated, in part, by the very speech of the protesters. For all the dictionary does is record *their* way of using the language.

Johnson didn't make all the changes that added up to the modern dictionary, of course. Others contributed. In 1773 a man called Kenrick published a dictionary that gave a fairly detailed system of pronunciation. The next year the Reverend James Barclay listed synonyms in his *Complete and Universal English Dictionary*.

In 1806, the American Noah Webster introduced some encyclopedic materials into his dictionary. Libraries and reference works were scarce then and Americans have always, apparently, loved something extra thrown in. After the first surprise they take it for granted and expect it. Therefore a few extras—tables of weights and measures, dates, brief biographies, and the like—have ever since been included in most American dictionaries.

Webster *did* set himself up as a reformer, particularly in the field of spelling, and some of his reforms (*labor* instead of *labour*, *traveled* instead of *travelled*, *theater* instead of *theatre*, etc.) were accepted. But most of them raised such a storm of protest that he withdrew them from subsequent editions.

English dictionary-making reached its high point in certain important respects in the publication of the monumental *Oxford English Dictionary*, which came out in separate parts from 1884 to 1928. This great work, designed and executed on historical principles, explores the origins and changes in meaning of almost every significant word then in the language. It also illustrates each change of meaning in a quotation used as an example. Preparing it required literally thousands of years of human lives, and it remains, and will remain, one of the proudest accomplishments of literary scholarship.

There are many special kinds of dictionaries in addition to the regular, standard ones. There are medical dictionaries, legal dictionaries, rhyming dictionaries, and dictionaries of slang, each serving a useful purpose. And as the language expands at such a terrific rate, and every field of learning seems to acquire new and specialized vocabularies, specialized dictionaries will probably increase. Except to the specialist, however, they have little value. The common reader will find little in them that concerns him or her that can't be found in a standard dictionary.

Among special dictionaries, two, perhaps, merit special mention. One of these is a dictionary of synonyms which groups words by similar meanings. Such dictionaries usually include antonyms as well. As mentioned before, most good standard dictionaries have lists of synonyms and some discussion when a number of identical or closely related meanings warrant it. Of course, a dictionary of synonyms can provide fuller discussions and more illustrations than the standard dictionaries can.

A thesaurus (the name come from a Greek word meaning "treasury") is a special form of a dictionary of synonyms. In a thesaurus, the words are grouped according to similar meanings, with the object of offering all possible synonyms or equivalents for all senses of a word. It does not, however, otherwise distinguish between them. For example, one thesaurus lists for *raw*: chilly, piercing, cutting; immature, crude, unripe, uncooked, unprepared; excoriated, galled, chafed; unskilled, untrained, green, inexperienced; wind-swept, exposed, bleak. After such an entry, there is a reference to other words which may offer further associations. Thus a thesaurus serves as a reminder for one who knows what the words mean but cannot recall the one wanted, or for one who wants a more exact expression than comes to mind. A thesaurus makes variety possible by bringing equivalents to mind. It helps one to get out of the rut of one's own familiar vocabulary.

A thesaurus can be bewildering, however. And, at best, it is a supplementary work.

The main thing is the dictionary. Anyone who is seriously interested in improving his or her vocabulary—which is to say mind, awareness, very self—must buy a dictionary and use it every day.

PRONUNCIATION KEY

aa	as in	cat, plaid
ah	as in	father, hearth, sergeant
air	as in	rare, air, prayer, there, wear, their
ate	as in	mate, straight, eight
ay	as in	gauge, way, steak, eh, obey, lane, rain, rein
aw	as in	tall, Utah, talk, fault, law, order, broad, fought
b	as in	book, hobby
ch	as in	chop, watch, righteous, question, nature
d	as in	day, ladder, pulled
e	as in	any, aesthetic, said, says, beg, leather, heifer, leopard, friend, bury
ee	as in	Caesar, evil, team, see, receive, people, key, machine, field, amoeba
eye	as in	aisle, aye, height, eye, ice, pie, buy, sky, lye, island, sigh
f	as in	fall, muffin, tough, physical
g	as in	gate, haggle, ghost, guard, catalogue
h	as in	happy, who
i	as in	England, been, ink, sieve, women, busy, build, hymn
ih	as in	attitude
ize	as in	lies, surprise, dyes, eyes
j	as in	graduate, judgment, ledge, soldier, cage, magic, exaggerate, jelly
k	as in	cook, account, saccharin, chronic, quick, liquor, acquaint, biscuit
l	as in	line, mellow
m	as in	calm, seam, limb, hammer, hymn
n	as in	know, now, runner, pneumonia, gnat
ng	as in	pink, hang, tongue
ngg	as in	linger
o	as in	beau, sew, note, road, toe, oh, brooch, soul, flow
oo	as in	maneuver, grew, move, wolf, canoe, ooze, look, troupe, should, rule, pull, flue, fruit
p	as in	pat, apple
r	as in	rat, carry, rhythm
s	as in	city, some, science, missile

sh	as in	ocean, machine, special, sugar, conscience, nauseous, ship, mansion, tissue, mission, mention, fuchsia
t	as in	talked, bought, tip, thyme
th	as in	think
u	as in	come, does, flood, couple, up
uh	as in	ability, mountain, system, dungeon, comical, parliament, gallop, porpoise, obvious, circus
v	as in	of, Stephen, victory, flivver
w	as in	choir, quiet, work
y	as in	union, hallelujah, you, confuse
z	as in	has, discern, scissors, zoo, dazzle, xylophone
zh	as in	garage, measure, division
'		is substituted for a vowel before a consonant to indicate that the vowel is to be pronounced only briefly; for example **comical** (KAHM uh k'l), **session** (SESH'n), **reason** (REE z'n).

Syllables shown in CAPITAL LETTERS are given main stress: **living** (LIV ing), **president** (PREZ ih d'nt), **reside** (rih ZIDE).

WORD-A-DAY
VOCABULARY
LIST

abbreviate (uh BREE vee ate) The -brev- in this word comes from the Latin *brevis*, meaning short, which is also the source of *brief*. Abbreviate thus means to make briefer, to make shorter by combining or omitting: you can abbreviate *dozen* as *doz.* and *quart* as *qt*.

   abbreviation (uh bree vee AY sh'n) is the noun, a shortened form of a word or phrase which stands for the whole: *Abbr. is the abbreviation for abbreviation;* or a reduction in length: *Some abbreviation of the speech was necessary because he didn't have enough time to deliver all of it.*

   abbreviated (uh BREE vee ay t'd), shortened: *She abbreviated the plot of the novel to "boy meets girl, boy loses girl, boy gets girl."*

abhorrent (aab HAWR 'nt; aab HAHR 'nt) The spelling of the word shows that it is related to *horror*. It means feeling horror, when used with *of*: *I was so abhorrent of snakes I would almost faint if I saw one;* or utterly opposed, when used with *to*: *Her casual disregard for the truth was abhorrent to his New England upbringing;* exciting horror, detestable: *The sight of blood was particularly abhorrent to him after the accident.*

   abhor (aab HAWR), to regard with horror or loathing.

   abhorrence (aab HAWR 'ns; aab HAHR 'ns), a feeling of extreme aversion: *I have an abhorrence of monster movies;* or the thing detested: *Monster movies are an abhorrence to me.*

abstract (ub STRAAKT) This word and its derivatives came from the Latin meaning to take away or separate. As a verb, it means exactly that. It can apply to the physical act of taking away when it means stealing: *He abstracted the damaging letters from the files.* But more often it refers to a mental act, considering a general object apart from special circumstances: *It is hard to abstract any one element in that picture—the drawing, the color or the com-*

51

position—which most appeals to me; or summarizing—that is, taking out the essential elements: *Abstract the main points of your speech and write them down for me.*

abstract (AAB straakt) used as a noun, with the emphasis on the first syllable, is a summary of a statement, document, or speech: *abstracts of articles in the medical journals.* More broadly, it concentrates in itself the essential qualities of anything larger or more general, or of several things. It is an essence or ideal, apart from any material basis: *She represented an abstract of all the qualities he admired in a woman. In the abstract* means without reference to particular circumstances or applications. *Abstract of title* is a legal term, the outline history of the title to a parcel of real estate.

abstract (either pronunciation) as an adjective means pertaining to the idea of something rather than to the thing itself, it is often opposed to concrete: *The number five is abstract, but five books is concrete; city is abstract, but New York is concrete. Abstract art* may be said to picture the meaning, for it is art which does not represent the appearance of specific objects. It uses only lines, colors, and forms to achieve its effects, to put across the *quality* of a thing, idea, or feeling.

abstraction (ub STRAAK sh'n), another noun meaning a general term or an idea, usually one not intended to lead to practical results. *Abstraction* refers more to an idea, *abstract* to an essence. *Abstraction* can also mean absent-mindedness: *He was in a state of such deep abstraction he failed to hear the doorbell;* or the act of taking away: *The abstraction of one element changes the nature of a chemical compound;* or a work of abstract art.

abstracted (ub STRAAK t'd), lost in thought, preoccupied.

accent (AAK sent) The root of this word is the Latin *cantus,* which means a singing; also related to *chant.* As in singing, the use of pitch and tone of voice is what makes one syllable in a word, or one word in a group, stand out above the others; it gives them the accent, or emphasis. *Accent* also refers to the mark used to indicate such emphasis: *Put the accent mark after "ac."* Accent may also mean a characteristic way of speaking: *Her French accent charmed the audience.* The regular stress in poetry or music is called the accent, although the sense of the words in poetry or an accent mark in music may call for special emphasis off the regular beat, *accentuation.*

accent (AK sent; aak SENT) as a verb means to emphasize in speaking or to mark with an accent in writing.

accentuate (aak SEN choo ate) is a slightly stronger verb, to emphasize clearly, to intensify: *Do you remember the song "You've got to Accentuate the Positive"?*

accolade (aak uh LADE) An award of honor: *The Purple Heart is an accolade*. This meaning developed out of the name for the ceremony used in conferring knighthood, which at one time consisted of embracing the candidate and then giving him a light blow on the shoulder with the flat of the sword. (The word comes by way of French and Italian from the Latin, to embrace about the neck.) It still means the ceremony of marking recognition of special merit.

acquiesce (aak wee ES) Related to *quiet;* to accept quietly; consent, agree, or comply passively. Although it implies no opposition, it does suggest submission rather than active agreement; often followed by *in: We acquiesced in his plans, although we were too tired to take much interest in them*.

    acquiescence (aak wee ES 'ns), act or condition of acquiescing; a silent submission: *Her silence showed her acquiescence*.

    acquiescent (aak wee ES 'nt), inclined or tending to yield; submissive. All of these words are derived from *quiescent* (kwy ES 'nt), being at rest, quiet or still; inactive or motionless.

activate (AAK tuh vate) To make active or more active, or to hasten reactions by various means. The last two meanings apply particularly to chemistry and physics. In general, then, it means to stimulate action by applying some new force or motive: *An army activates a unit by assigning it troops and equipment necessary for war strength and training*.

    activation (aak tuh VAY sh'n), the act or process of activating.

    activator (AAK tuh vay t'r), the person, thing, or process which activates.

adduce (uh DOOS; uh DYOOS) The root of this word, *-duce,* comes from the Latin *ducere,* to lead (Mussolini was *Il Duce,* the leader). Combined with *ad-,* meaning *to,* it means to bring toward or forward, not in a physical sense but mentally; to bring forward in argument, to offer as having bearing on a case: *He adduced several instances of their disobedience as reasons for punishing them*.

    Deduce, educe, conduce, induce, and *reduce* have the same root. *Deduce* means to conclude from something already known— that is, to lead *from; educe,* to draw forth or bring out, to lead *out of; conduce,* to lead or contribute to a result (followed by *to*), to lead together; *induce,* or lead or move by persuasion or influence, to lead *into; reduce,* to bring down to a smaller extent, size, amount or number, to lead *back*.

affable (AAF uh b'l) Approachable, polite, friendly. The source of the word is from the Latin, meaning to speak to. From this it has come to mean easy to speak to, therefore an agreeable or pleasant person or manner: *His affable greeting put the visitor at ease at once.*

    affability (aaf uh BIL uh tee) is the noun for the quality or state of being affable: *His co-workers marveled at his constant affability, even under pressure.*

affinity (uh FIN uh tee) A natural liking for or attraction to a person or thing: *She seems to have an affinity for unappreciated artists;* the person for whom such a liking is felt; or an inherent likeness or agreement, as between things, a close resemblance or connection: *Certain foods seem to have an affinity for each other, like ham and eggs or pancakes and syrup;* or a relationship by marriage—that is, not a blood relationship. All the meanings of this word are based on the idea of a relationship; the last meaning, although not the most familiar, was the original one.

    affinitive (uh FIN uh tiv), closely related.

affluent (AAF loo 'nt) The *-flu-* shows that the root of this word is the Latin one meaning flow. Affluent means flowing freely, therefore abundant or rich: *His affluent mode of living finally made his employers suspicious that he had some irregular source of income. America has been called "the affluent society."*

    affluence (AAF loo 'ns), an abundance of material goods, wealth; or an abundant supply, as of thoughts, words, etc.: *The affluence of the community attracted a number of exclusive shops. Rich, affluent, opulent,* and *wealthy* all indicate abundance of possessions. *Rich* is the most general word; it may imply that possessions are newly acquired. *Wealthy* suggests permanence, stability, and appropriate surroundings. *Affluent* and *opulent* both suggest the possession of great wealth. Affluent especially implies a handsome income and free spending; *opulent* suggests display or luxuriousness.

aggregate (adj.: AAG ruh g't; noun; AAG ruh gate) As an adjective, this means formed by a collection of parts into a mass or sum total; combined: *the aggregate amount turned in by the collec-*

tors. As a noun, it means a sum, mass, or collection of parts: *The aggregate of the donations turned in was beyond their expectations*. From this comes the common phrase, *in the aggregate,* taken together, considered as a whole.

As a verb, *aggregate* means to bring together, to collect into one mass or body, or to amount to: *The collection aggregated to $500*.

aggregation (aag ruh GAY sh'n), a combined whole; the act of collecting into an unorganized whole: *The aggregation of a large enough group was a difficult job;* the state of being so collected.

congregate, to come together, and *congregation,* an assemblage or the act of coming together, are related to *aggregate*. Both groups of words are based on the Latin word, *gregare,* meaning collect.

agility (uh JIL uh tee) The power of moving quickly and easily; nimbleness. It may apply to either mind or body: *Speed and agility are essential for a tennis player. The agility of his intellect allowed him to follow a number of interests at the same time*.

agile (AAJ 'l), quick and light in movement; active, lively.

agilely (AAJ uh lee), in an agile manner: *She seemed to move as agilely as a cat.*

alienate (ALE yuh nate) This obviously comes from alien, based on the Latin *alienus,* from *alius,* another. An alien is a foreigner or stranger, someone not eligible for the privileges of a citizen; he is excluded. Thus, to alienate is to estrange, to make indifferent where feeling had formerly existed, to separate or turn away: *Her odd behavior gradually alienated all her friends*. In law it means to convey, as title, property, or other right, to another: *He agreed to alienate certain lands, to be paid for over a period of years*.

alienation (ale yuh NAY sh'n), a withdrawal or estrangement, as of feeling or the affections: *Alienation of affections may be the basis for a lawsuit;* in law, the act of alienating.

alien (ALE y'n) is an adjective meaning foreign, strange, not belonging to one; or it can have the stronger meaning of hostile or opposed: *His ideas were alien to our system of beliefs*.

alienable (ALE yuh nuh b'l), capable of being sold or transferred—that is, of being given to another.

alienage (ALE yuh n'j), the state of being an alien; the legal standing of an alien, a noncitizen.

The *unalienable rights* referred to in the Declaration of

Independence are those which cannot be transferred to another, even voluntarily. Nowadays the more common term would be *inalienable*.

allegation (aal uh GAY sh'n) A statement offered as a plea, an excuse, or a justification; a statement made without any proof; an assertion made by a party in a legal proceeding which he undertakes to prove. An allegation is not as strong as a statement or declaration, for it suggests some doubt; however, it also implies a readiness on the part of the person making it to back it up: *The jury could not accept the allegation of Communism without unquestionable evidence.*

allege (uh LEJ) is the verb related to allegation. It means to declare with positiveness; affirm; assert. To allege may be to declare before a court or elsewhere, as if upon oath; assert without proof: *He alleged that the other two men also took part in the crime, although they denied it.*

alleged (uh LEJD), an adjective formed from the verb, meaning asserted to be true: *the alleged offense, an alleged marriage;* questionably true or as described: *the alleged music that youngsters dance to nowadays.*

allegedly (uh LEJ 'd lee), according to allegation: *He was allegedly at home when the shooting took place.*

alleviate (uh LEE vee ate) To make something easier to endure; lessen; lighten. The core of the word is from the Latin *levis*, light. Thus to alleviate is to make a mental or physical burden lighter: *Many drugs are now available to alleviate pain. The new building program will help to alleviate the housing pressure.*

alleviation (uh lee vee AY sh'n), the act of alleviating; or something that alleviates: *The doctor was dedicated to the alleviation of pain.*

alleviative (uh LEE vee ay t'v), serving to alleviate; something that alleviates: *A criminal would consider a life sentence alleviative compared with capital punishment.*

alleviatory (uh LEE vee uh tawr ee), alleviative.

Alleviate, mitigate, allay, assuage all connote relief from some painful state.

Mitigate is to lessen in force or intensity, to soften; *allay,* to quiet (as tumult, fear, suspicion), to put at rest; *assuage* to make milder or less severe, to appease or pacify.

Alleviate is the opposite of *aggravate* (from *gravis,* heavy), to make something worse or more serious; that is, to make the burden heavier.

allocate (AAL uh kate) To set apart for a particular purpose; assign or allot: *Certain plots were allocated for housing, others for commercial buildings;* to fix the place of. The Latin *locare*, to place, is the root of the word, from which locate also comes. Locate is simply to discover the place or location of, to establish in a place, while allocate is to place apart.

   allocation (aal uh KAY sh'n), the act of allocating or apportionment; the share or proportion allocated: *The allocation of tickets aroused complaint from some who thought they had not been given enough.*

ambiguity (aam buh GYOO uh tee) Doubtfulness or uncertainty of meaning: *The ambiguity of certain poems may frustrate readers;* or a word or expression capable of being interpreted in more than one way: *It is an ambiguity to say that an insect is a feeling creature.* Also **ambiguousness** (am BIG yew 's n's).

   ambiguous (aam BIG yoo 's), open to various interpretations, having a double meaning of doubtful or uncertain nature; lacking clearness or definiteness: *She felt I was being deliberately ambiguous so as to confuse her.*

   ambiguously (aam BIG yoo 's lee), in an ambiguous manner. *Equivocal* and *ambiguous* both describe what is not clear in meaning, but something *ambiguous* does not have to be purposely misleading, while something *equivocal* is usually intended to deceive.

ameliorate (uh MEEL yuh rate) This is from the Latin *meliorare*, to make better. It means to make or grow better, to improve, but is a more formal word than improve: *He dedicated himself to ameliorating the ills caused by poverty and disease in the slums.*

   amelioration (uh meel yuh RAY sh'n), the act of ameliorating; the resulting state: *the amelioration of his condition after he took the medicine.*

   ameliorative (uh MEEL yuh ray t'v; uh MEEL yuh ruh t'v), tending to ameliorate.

   ameliorable (uh MEEL yuh ruh b'l), capable of being ameliorated: *These problems are ameliorable with the help of the right kind of equipment.*

   ameliorator (uh MEEL yuh ray t'r), one who ameliorates. *Improve* and *ameliorate* both mean to make better, but *improve* implies remedying a lack or a felt need in a state not necessarily bad; *ameliorate*, making unsatisfactory conditions better.

amenable (uh MEE nuh b'l; uh MEN uh b'l) Disposed or ready to answer, yield, or submit; *I am amenable to any reasonable suggestion;* liable to be called to account, answerable: *His argument did not seem amenable to the rules of logic.* The word also has the meaning of liable or exposed to a charge, claim, etc., but this usage is not as common as the others. The idea of yielding or submission to authority comes from the Latin root, *minare,* to drive, as animals.

amenability (uh mee nuh BIL uh tee; uh men uh BIL uh tee) the quality or state of being amenable; *her amenability to a change of plans.*

amenableness (uh MEE nuh b'l n's; uh MEN uh b'l n's), the state of being amenable.

amenably (uh MEE nuh blee; uh MEN uh blee), in an amenable manner. *She agreed so amenably that I would have never thought her angry.*

apathy (AAP uh thee) This comes directly from the Greek *apatheia,* meaning insensibility. It means lack of feeling, the absence or suppression of passion, emotion, or excitement; a lack of interest in things which others find moving or exciting: *Her apathy toward the things she used to be fond of alarmed her family.*

apathetic (aap uh THET ik), having or showing little or no emotion; indifferent: *He was apathetic to all attempts to engage his interest.*

apathetically (aap uh THET uh k'lee), in an apathetic manner. *The child answered so apathetically I thought he was sick.* *Sympathy, empathy,* and *antipathy* all come from the same root, *pathos,* meaning suffering, pain, intense feeling. *A-* in the Greek is a negative prefix; thus *apathy* means no pain or feeling. *Syn-* means with, and combines to form *sympathy,* meaning agreement in feeling, as between persons or on the part of one person with respect to another. *En-,* in or into, combines to make *empathy,* a mental entering into the feeling or spirit of a person or thing. *Anti-,* against, makes *antipathy* a feeling against, aversion.

apropos (aap ruh PO) This has been taken over from the French phrase, *à propos,* and means the same: with reference or regard, in respect (followed by of): *Apropos of what you said yesterday, I completely agree.* It may be used by itself to mean by the way: *Apropos, I wanted to tell you.* As an adjective it means opportune, pertinent: *She took great pains to choose gifts apropos to the occasion.*

Apropos sounds like and is related to the adjective *appro-*

priate. But *apropos* comes originally from a Latin word meaning purpose, whereas *appropriate* comes from one meaning one's own.

arbiter (AHR buh t'r) A person given the power to decide points in dispute; one who has the sole or absolute power of judging or determining: *A parliamentarian is an arbiter essential to the smooth conduct of a formal meeting.* An arbiter differs from a judge in that his or her decision in a disagreement can be personal and is not subject to review.

An **arbitrator** (AHR buh tray t'r) is a person chosen to decide a dispute. Although it used to be synonymous with *arbiter,* it has come to suggest one with a more tactful and diplomatic approach, intent on bringing opposed parties together. This is partly due to the popular association of arbitrator with the settling of labor disputes. Therefore, an arbitrator is no longer likely to be arbitrary or dictatorial.

arbitrament (ahr BIT ruh m'nt) refers to the act of arbitration. It is also the decision of the arbitrator. It is not a common word.

arbitrary (AHR buh trair ee) usually refers to a situation or a judgement that is final and not based on careful consideration. It has strong overtones of unreasonable: *His arbitrary decision to fire the staff threw everyone into a panic.*

arbitrate (AHR buh trate) means to determine or to act as a judge in: *They asked a friend to arbitrate their dispute.*

arbitration (ahr buh TRA sh'n) is a law term referring to the settlement out of court, by an impartial judge acceptable to all parties.

articulate (adj.: ahr TIK yuh l't; verb: ahr TIK yuh late) Used as an adjective, this means clear, distinct, clearly uttered: *Each syllable was beautifully articulate;* capable of speech: *Man is an articulate animal;* or having joints, made up of segments: *Vertebrate animals have articulate structures.* This last meaning shows the source in the Latin *articulatus,* divided into joints. From describing purely physical things, articulate has taken on broader meanings. Recently it has come to suggest communicating clearly and well: *A public relations man must be articulate.*

As a verb, it means to say distinctly; to unite by a joint or joints: *a well-articulated plan.*

articulation (ahr tik yuh LAY sh'n), the act or process of articulating speech; the act of jointing; or a jointed state or formation: *Medical students study the articulation of the skeleton.*

articulately (ahr TIK yuh l't lee), in an articulate manner.

articulateness (ahr TIK yuh l't n's), the quality or state of being articulate: *Articulateness was the senator's greatest asset in his campaigns.*

assimilate (uh SIM uh late) The Latin root, *similis,* like, shows that this word is related to similar. The first, and still current meaning is to make similar, followed by *to* or *with: We must try to assimilate our way of thinking to theirs.* But the more common one is to take in or absorb as one's own: *He wanted to assimilate as much information as he could in the short time allowed him.* In physiology, it is to convert something into a substance suitable for being absorbed into the system: *In the patient's weakened condition, he could assimilate only liquids.* The word may also be used without an object, as in reference to instruction: *She assimilates so quickly she can cover twice as much ground as the average student in the same time;* or absorption: *Some substances assimilate more easily than others into the circulatory system.*

assimilation (uh sim uh LAY sh'n), the act or process of assimilating, or the state or condition of being assimilated. In sociology, this has the special meaning of the merging of cultural traits—such as habits, attitudes, etc.—from groups of different national or racial backgrounds. It is distinguished from biological intermixture: *You can see the effects of assimilation by comparing the habits of first-generation immigrants with those of their children.*

assimilable (uh SIM uh luh b'l), capable of being assimilated.

assimilative (uh SIM uh lay t'v), characterized by assimilation; assimilating.

It is a common mistake to pronounce these words as if the core were simulate. *Assimilate* and *simulate* are both derived from the Latin *similis,* and have a related meaning: to assume or have the appearance of, to make a pretense of. But simulate suggests an intent to deceive; assimilate does not.

atrophy (AAT ruh fee) As a noun, this means a wasting away of the body, or of an organ or part, from defective nutrition or other causes: *The girl's confinement to a wheelchair caused a progressive atrophy of her leg muscles.*

As a verb, the meaning is to undergo or cause to undergo wasting away, as from lack of nutrition or disuse: *She began to*

*fear her mind would atrophy in her enforced solitude. His way of
living could atrophy the liver.*

atrophied (AAT ruh feed), exhibiting or affected with atrophy;
wasted: *an atrophied limb.*

attest (uh TEST) This comes from a Latin word meaning to bear
witness. Its relationship to testify and testimony is apparent. It
means to bear witness to, certify, declare to be true or genuine,
and especially to affirm in an official capacity: *His own broad
experience enabled him to attest the accuracy of the young
man's statements;* to give proof or evidence of: *The portrait
attested her beauty;* or to certify to the genuineness a of document by signing as a witness: *You must have a notary public
attest to that deed.*

attestation (aat es TAY sh'n), act of attesting; or an attesting
declaration, testimony, evidence: *His attestation of his employ-
ee's previous honesty helped to lighten the penalty.*

attribute (uh TRIB yoot) To consider as belonging: *They attributed much of his great skill in swimming to his training;* regard
as having been caused or brought about by: *She attributed his
silence to his preoccupation with the problems on his mind.*

Attribute, ascribe, and *impute* all imply regarding something as having definite origin, the first two as having originated
from a definite person or cause. *Attribute* is somewhat more
complimentary, possibly because of its association with tribute,
while *ascribe* is neutral: *to attribute advancement in one's
profession to intelligence and industry; to ascribe an illness to
infection. Impute* has uncomplimentary associations. It usually
suggests blaming or accusing someone or something as a cause:
He imputed evil motives to a desire for revenge.

attribute (AAT ruh byoot), the noun, is pronounced differently.
It is something considered as belonging; a quality, character,
characteristic, or property: *Her physical attributes were so striking as to attract every eye in the room.*

attribution (aat ruh BYOO sh'n), the act of attributing or
ascribing; that which is ascribed: *We heard about the attribution
of the unsigned article to a well-known scholar.*

attributive (uh TRIB yuh t'v), pertains to an attribute, especially an adjective or adverb preceding the word it modifies; or, as
a noun, a word expressing an attribute.

attributively (uh TRIB yuh t'v lee), in an attributive manner.

audacity (aw DAAS uh tee) Boldness or daring, with an implication of recklessness: *Their audacity in the face of danger inspired the rest of the group;* or insolence: *His audacity to his superiors called for disciplinary measures.*

Audacity suggests an open disregard for convention or moral restraint; effrontery; a shameless and impudent boldness.

audacious (aw DAY sh's), bold or daring; spirited, adventurous: *an audacious soldier;* reckless in wrongdoing, impudent, and presumptuous: *an audacious robbery.*

audaciously (aw DAY sh's lee), in an audacious manner.

augment (awg MENT) Coming from the Latin meaning to increase, this means to make larger, or enlarge in size or extent: *It was necessary to augment the supplies in order to feed additional members of the party;* to become greater: *The painting augmented in value to almost double its original price.*

augmentation (awg men TAY sh'n), the act of augmenting, an augmented state, or that by which anything is augmented: *Correcting papers brought a small but welcome augmentation to his income.*

augmentative (awg MEN tuh t'v), serving to augment.

Increase, enlarge, and *augment* are often interchangeable, but *increase* is a broader term—to make greater in quantity, size, duration or value—and less formal. *Augment* implies a substantial increase, especially from some outside addition. *Enlarge* applies more specifically to something which has dimensions or capacity.

auspicious (aw SPISH 's) Of good omen, predicting success, favorable. The word comes from the Latin *auspex,* a seer who in ancient times interpreted the future or predicted success or failure of a project from the behavior and movement of birds. The unfavorable association has been lost, however, so that the term now implies fortunate or prosperous circumstances: *This auspicious union of two great families.*

auspiciously (aw SPISH 's lee), in an auspicious manner: *The opening session went auspiciously.*

auspiciousness (aw SPISH 's n's), favorable conditions or prospects.

auspices (AW spis 's), favoring influence or patronage. This is almost always used in the plural, although a singular form exists and is acceptable: *Under the auspices of such a socially prominent group of hostesses, the charity ball was bound to be a success.*

austerity (aw STAIR uh tee) This comes from a Greek word meaning to parch or dry, but it is used in an extended sense to apply to a manner or way of life which is severe or harsh. It implies self-discipline and moral strictness: *The austerity of her home gave no indication of her great wealth.*

Austerity, hardship, privation all suggest conditions difficult to endure. *Hardship* applies where extreme and painful effort is required to withstand physical or mental discomfort, and *privation* where an absence of necessities exists. *Austerity* implies deliberate control and also a possible choice.

austere (aw STEER), harsh in manner, forbidding: *His austere appearance frightened her;* severe in restraining oneself: *Austere as he was in taking care of his own physical needs, he insisted that she have every available comfort;* sober; severely simple, unornamented: *austere language.*

austerely (aw STEER lee), in an austere manner.

axiom (AAK see 'm) A recognized truth; an established and universally accepted principle or rule: *One of the axioms of sound business practice is plowing back the profits;* in logic or mathematics, a proposition assumed without proof for the sake of studying the consequences: *It is an axiom that the whole is greater than its parts.*

axiomatic (aak see uh MAT ik), self-evident; pertaining to or the nature of an axiom.

axiomatically (aak see uh MAT ik'lee), in an axiomatic manner. *Axiom, aphorism, maxim, adage,* and *proverb* all express the idea of a self-evident general truth, but none has quite the force of *axiom* as a basic proposition to which everyone agrees. An *aphorism* is a brief, effectively expressed saying which conveys a general truth or feeling. A *maxim* is a similarly short striking statement of a generally accepted truth, usually relating to conduct or practical concerns. An *adage* is a long-current saying expressing a familiar truth or useful thought; a *proverb* is essentially the same, especially if it is stated in homely, vivid language.

belligerent (buh LIJ uh r'nt) Warlike, given to waging war, of warlike character or attitude: *His tone was so belligerent it frightened her;* or pertaining to war or those engaged in war: *Representatives of the belligerent nations agreed to an exploratory conference.* As a noun, the word refers to a state or nation at war or a member of the military forces of such a state: *As a belligerent in World War II, Italy claimed certain rights.*

belligerence (buh LIJ uh r'ns), warlike nature, or the act of carrying on war: *The belligerence of the exchanges between the two countries pointed to an early declaration of war.*

belligerency (buh LIJ uh r'n see), position or status as a belligerent, or the state of being actually engaged in war: *Because of a failure of communications, the belligerency of the tiny state was in doubt for twenty-four hours.* This word may also be used interchangeably with belligerence in the sense of having an aggressive attitude.

Bellicose, coming from the same Latin root (meaning war) as *belligerent,* also means inclined to war or warlike. It should properly be applied to nations or peoples, but has come to refer to persons inclined to threaten to fight. There is scarcely any distinction between the two words, except for the formal applications of *belligerent* in international law. Actually, *belligerent* is much more commonly used than *bellicose.*

beneficent (buh NEF uh s'nt) Doing good, causing good to be done; kindly in action or purpose: *Her beneficent contributions to the settlement house did much to help others.*

beneficence (buh NEF uh s'ns), the doing of good; active kindness or charity; *The beneficence of the king to his subjects on his son's birth caused rejoicing.*

beneficently (buh NEF uh s'nt lee), in a beneficent manner. *Benevolent* (buh NEV uh l'nt), desiring to do good for others, is often confused with *beneficent* because of the first two syllables (bene- means well), and the similar meanings. The distinction can be seen in the third syllable: *-fic-* is from the Latin meaning to do, *-vol-* from the Latin for to wish. Thus *beneficent* is well-doing, *benevolent* well-wishing: *He expressed his benevolent feelings through the beneficent gift of his country estate as a rehabilitation center.*

benign (bih NINE) A kind of gracious disposition, as applied to people: *His benign manner made them feel that they could confide in him;* favorable, as applied to circumstances. *The benign weather encouraged them to spend the whole week at the shore.*

benignant (bih NIG n'nt), kind or gracious, but more suggestive of condescension than benign: *Unusually benignant in the treatment of his serfs, the lord was considered foolishly generous.* Benignant is related to *benign* as *malignant* is to *malign,* their opposites in meaning.

benignity (bih NIG nuh tee), the quality of being benign, kindness.

benignly (bih NINE lee), in a benign manner.

bizarre (bih ZAHR) Strikingly unusual in appearance, style, or general character; out of the ordinary: *Some people thought beatniks dressed in a bizarre fashion;* out of keeping. Usually the word suggests something peculiar: *bizarre clothes, bizarre behavior, bizarre circumstances.*

This word, of Basque origin, has nothing to do with *bazaar.* Although it sounds the same, *bazaar* is Persian, and it refers to a market place where goods are sold, or a sale of miscellaneous articles for some special purpose: *The school held a bazaar to raise money for athletic equipment.*

blatant (BLAY t'nt) From some form of the word *bleat,* its original meaning was noisy. It now means offensively noisy or intrusive in any way (as uncontrolled noise would be); in coarse taste, in a vulgar or inconsiderate manner: *His blatant disregard of common courtesy was extremely embarrassing to the other guests. Blatant ignorance is her curse.*

    blatancy (BLAY t'n see), blatant quality; anything blatant: *The blatancy of his conceit prevented him from advancing as fast as he might have otherwise.*

    blatantly (BLAY t'nt lee), in a blatant manner.

bombastic (bahm BAAS tik) An adjective meaning high-flown or high-sounding, descriptive of a person or of language. Its source is a word meaning padding (of cotton or other soft material), once used as stuffing for garments. Thus it has come to refer to inflated language or to a pompous person, one artificially over-stuffed. The slang expression *stuffed shirt* refers to one who is bombastic: *His language was bombastic, and his speech was absurd.*

    bombast (BAHM baast), high-sounding words, speech too pretentious for the occasion: *Looking at the list of speakers on the program he feared he was in for an evening of bombast.*

    bombastically (bahm BAAS tuh k'lee), in a bombastic manner.

brusque (BRUSK) Blunt and rough in manner; short; abrupt; *His brusque way of speaking kept his colleagues from trying to be friendly.* The source of this word is probably Latin for butcher's-broom, a prickly kind of shrub actually used for making brooms. Thus, there is a feeling of sharpness in brusque.

    brusqueness (BRUSK n's), the quality or state of being brusque.

    brusquely (BRUSK lee), in a brusque manner.

    Bluff, blunt, and *curt* also convey abruptness in manner;

but *bluff* suggests unintentional roughness, accompanied by heartiness and good-nature; *blunt,* a lack of polish and consideration; and *curt* an undue briefness or sharpness.

cadence (KAY d'ns) A rhythmic flow, as in poetry, or the beat of any rhythmical movement; *Milton's cadences have often been compared to an organ roll;* the fall or the general modulation of the voice in speaking: *The monotonous cadence of the speaker's voice was putting him to sleep;* in music, a sequence of notes indicating a conclusion; from the Latin *cadere,* meaning, literally, to fall. Sometimes it is spelled **cadency** (KAY d'n see).

    cadent (KAY d'nt), having cadence, or rhythmical fall.

    cadenza (kuh DEN zuh), a musical term for a showy passage near the end of an operatic aria or of a movement of a concerto.

candid (KAAN did) In its original Latin, this word meant white. From this it has come to mean pure, clear, open, fair, and most commonly now, frank or outspoken: *His candid appraisal of the alternatives made the issues much clearer to them.*

    candidly (KAAN did lee), in a candid manner.

    candidness (KAAN did n's), openness, frankness, sincerity.

    Candidate is derived from candid's original meaning. Aspirants for public office in ancient Rome wore white togas, hence they were those clothed in white.

    Candid, frank, open, outspoken all suggest freedom and boldness in speaking. *Candid* implies fairness and sincerity in expression, even at the occasional cost of unpleasantness. (The phrase, *my candid opinion,* is likely to alert the listener's defenses.) *Frank* suggests an unreserved expression of opinion or feeling: *frank delight, frank disapproval. Open* implies lack of reserve or concealment: *His open commitment to an unpopular course worried his supporters;* outspoken, freedom in speaking even when inappropriate: *Her outspoken criticism of the chairman's statement caused some raised eyebrows.*

capitulate (kuh PICH uh late) To surrender unconditionally or on agreed-upon terms. The source of the word is the Latin *capitulare,* to draw up under chapter headings, hence the modern meaning of the word. Its primary use is in a military sense: *The enemy capitulated when it became obvious that reinforcements could not reach them;* but it is also used in a freer, less formal sense of giving in under pressure: *She capitulated to his insistent pleas to leave the country*.

capitulation (kuh pich uh LAY sh'n), the act of capitulating, or the statement of the terms of surrender. This can also mean a summary or enumeration: *a capitulation of the subjects discussed*.

careen (kuh REEN) The most common meaning of this word in ordinary speech is to lean, sway, or tip to one side. This is an expansion of its more specific meaning, to cause a ship to lie on its side—as for repairs—or to cause it to heel over. Popularly, it is applied to unsteady movement, either walking or in a vehicle: *He careened drunkenly from table to door. The car careened dangerously as the driver lost control*.

Career (kuh REER) is sometimes confused with careen because they both mean to move or run rapidly: *He careered purposefully down the road in pursuit, causing those in his way to scatter for their own safety*. The distinguishing element is one of control—*careening* is likely to be involuntary, *careering* intentional.

cataclysm (KAAT uh kliz'm) This word has developed from a description of a specific physical event to a generalized application. Its source is the Greek word for flood, and it originally meant a deluge. It is sometimes applied to the Biblical flood. Then it came to signify a violent physical action producing changes in the earth's surface. Now, finally, it refers to any violent upheaval, especially a social or political one, which is the sense in which it is most commonly used today: *The French Revolution was one of the greatest social cataclysms of modern history. The eruption of the volcano Krakatoa in the last century was a true cataclysm*.

cataclysmic (kaat uh KLIZ mik), pertaining to or resulting from a cataclysm. A variant of this is **cataclysmal** (kaat uh KLIZ m'l).

chicanery (shih KAY nuh ree) Trickery, sharp practice, quibbling with an intent to mislead or to obscure the truth: *His chicanery in business dealings came to light when his victims began clamoring for repayment*.

chicane (shih KANE) as a noun is a synonym for chicanery. As a verb it means to trick by chicanery, or to use chicanery. This is not a common word, however, and is seldom used in ordinary conversation or writing.

clairvoyant (klair VOY 'nt) Having the power of seeing objects or actions beyond the natural range of vision. It comes from two words meaning *clear* and *see,* thus, clear-seeing. But it is more than seeing clearly, for it suggests perception beyond the senses, a second sight: *As events turned out, her earlier advice made her seem clairvoyant.*

The word is also a noun, meaning a clairvoyant person.

clairvoyance (klair VOY 'ns), the power to see beyond the natural range of vision; by extension, a quick intuitive knowledge of things; penetration: *Some business newsletters would have you believe their forecasters are possessed of clairvoyance on future trends.*

clairvoyantly (klair VOY 'nt lee), in a clairvoyant manner.

clandestine (klaan DES t'n) Secret, private, concealed, usually with the implication of craftiness or deception: *Their clandestine scheme to manipulate the funds was suddenly exposed by one of their accomplices.*

clandestinely (klaan DES t'n lee), in a clandestine manner.

clandestineness (klaan DES t'n n's), the state of being clandestine: *the clandestineness of their meetings.*

coercion (ko ER sh'n) The act of compelling or restraining by force, law, or authority, or the power of doing so: *the coercion of his family; He was forced to return the property by legal coercion.* The word implies resistance being overcome by force of some kind.

coerce (ko ERS), to compel by forcible action: *Enjoyment cannot be coerced.*

coercive (ko ER s'v), serving or tending to coerce: *His coercive methods with his subordinates made him heartily disliked.*

coercively (ko ER s'v lee), in a coercive manner.

coerciveness (ko ER s'v n's), exerting coercion.

coercible (ko ER suh b'l), capable of being coerced.

coherence (ko HEER 'ns) The *-her-* root is the same as in adherence, and means stick. The word signifies a sticking together, therefore a union of parts; or a natural or logical connection: *The coherence of the argument gave it great persuasive force;* consistency.

cohere (ko HEER), the verb, meaning to stick together, be united; or to be naturally or logically connected: *The elements of a structure must cohere to give it strength;* or to agree.

coherent (ko HEER 'nt) sticking together, consistent, logical: *He usually speaks in a notably coherent fashion.*

incoherent (in ko HEER 'nt) means the opposite of coherent: *His explanation was so incoherent we couldn't make head or tail of it.*

Coherence and *cohesion* both imply a sticking together. *Cohesion* is usually applied in a physical sense of literally sticking together, while *coherence* is more often applied to order and consistency of thought or statements. The same kind of distinction exists between *adhesion* and *adherence*.

The difference between *adherence* and *coherence* is that the former implies a simple sticking to: *his adherence to party principles;* the latter, a sticking *together* to form a whole: *the coherence of all parts of the composition.*

collusion (kuh LOO zh'n) A secret agreement for fraudulent purpose; conspiracy. In law it refers specifically to a secret understanding between two or more persons to the disadvantage of another, or with the appearance of having opposite interests although actually in agreement. The word comes from the Latin for playing together.

collusive (kuh LOO s'v), involving collusion, fraudulently planned together. *They thought up a collusive scheme to freeze out the other two partners.*

collusively (kuh LOO s'v lee), in a collusive manner. *They planned collusively in working out their plot.*

collude (kuh LOOD), to act together through a secret understanding. *Collusion* and *coöperation* both refer to acting together, usually for mutual benefit, but coöperation has no suggestion of fraud or secrecy.

commensurate (kuh MEN shuh r't) The Latin *mensuratus,* measured, is the source of this word, which means having the same measure, equal in extent or duration; corresponding; proportionate: *His pay will be commensurate with that of the others.*

commensurable (kuh MEN shuh ruh b'l), having a common measure: *Business property and residential property are usually not commensurable in terms of price.*

commensurability (kuh men shuh ruh BIL uh tee), correspondence; possession of a common measure.

Commensurate differs from *proportionate* slightly because it suggests an exact proportion or measurable equality between the things compared. *Proportionate* is more general, implying a relationship in accordance with some assumed standard: *His efforts did not bring proportionate rewards.*

complement (KAHM pluh m'nt) That which makes complete or perfect: *Experiment is a necessary complement of study in the physical sciences. Coffee is a complement to a good dinner;* full quantity or complete allowance: *The school was handicapped by not having its full complement of teachers.* The word has a military application, referring to the number of men required to fill out a company or man a ship: *Sailing was delayed until enough crew replacements could be found to make up the complement.* It also means either of two parts needed to complete the whole.

As a verb it is to complete or form a complement to: *Your accessories complement your suit beautifully.*

complementary (kahm pluh MEN tuh ree), forming a complement, or complementing each other: *Gilbert and Sullivan had complementary talents.* Complementary colors in physics are pairs which, when mixed in equal proportions, produce white or gray light, as blue and yellow, or purple and orange.

complemental (kahm pluh MEN t'l), of the nature of or pertaining to a complement.

Complement and *supplement* both mean to make an addition to something; but *complement* is making up a deficiency, rendering something complete, while *supplement* suggests a simple addition to something which does not depend on it for completeness.

Complement is sometimes confused with *compliment,* an expression of praise or admiration: *He paid her the compliment of asking her advice;* or one of formal courtesy: *The champagne came with the compliments of the house.*

compunction (kum PUNK sh'n) The *-punc-* part of this word is from the Latin *pungere,* to prick. It means a pricking of conscience, regret for wrongdoing or causing pain to another, remorse: *She was overcome with compunction at having offended him.* Modern usage does not give as much strength to this word as it used to have; it is rather freely used to express passing regret for some minor breach or injury, very often in a negative phrase: *I had no compunction about breaking the appointment.*

conciliate (kun SIL ee ate) To overcome distrust or hostility by soothing means: *He decided the best way to conciliate his father would be to offer to pay for the damage to the car;* to win or gain favor: *To conciliate the suspicious child she regularly brought gifts;* to reconcile or promote agreement: *A successful arbitrator is skillful at conciliating hostile negotiators.*

conciliation (kun sil ee AY sh'n), the process of conciliating, or the state of being conciliated: *He devoted all his efforts toward concilation of the two factions.*

conciliatory (kun SIL ee uh tawr ee), tending to conciliate: *He decided to take a conciliatory approach to the differences between them.*

conciliator (kun SIL ee ay t'r), an arbitrator or peacemaker, one who conciliates.

conciliatoriness (kun SIL ee uh tawr ee n's), disposition to conciliate or be conciliated: *His unexpected conciliatoriness gave them hope of reaching an agreement sooner than they had anticipated.*

Conciliate, appease, and *propitiate* all imply trying to obtain or preserve peace. *Conciliate* suggests trying to win over someone by displaying willingness to be fair. *Appease* conveys the idea of anxiety, with a willingness to make undue concessions, and has acquired unfavorable overtones since dealings with Hitler. *Propitiate* is to admit a fault and to try to make amends.

connive (kuh NIVE) The Latin source of this word means to shut the eyes. A man who connives shuts his eyes to wrongdoing. He avoids noticing what he should condemn but secretly approves. Thus he really contributes to it by not acting to prevent it. In this sense the word is followed by *at: He connived at their plan to throw the blame on John.* In the sense of secret coöperation, it is followed by *with: He connived with them in their plan.* The word is sometimes used to apply to innocent activities, as in conniving to get someone out of the way for a surprise party, but there is still the implication of conspiracy.

connivance (kun NIVE 'ns), avoidance of seeing or making wrongdoing known. It may involve passive consent or secret cooperation: *With the connivance of the bookkeeper, discovery of the embezzlement was delayed long enough for the secretary to get out of the country.*

conniver (kuh NIVE 'r), one who connives. This may refer to one who connives at a specific act, or who habitually behaves in a conniving fashion: *He had an unwholesome reputation as a conniver in his business dealings.*

consummate (KAHN suh mate) To bring to completion or perfection: *The settling of these troublesome details will enable us to* *consummate the transaction today*. It commonly means to complete marriage by sexual intercourse.

consummate (kun SUM m't), the adjective, is pronounced differently. It means complete or perfect; supremely qualified; of highest quality: *His consummate genius dwarfed the work of his contemporaries*. The *summa* of *summa cum laude*, with highest honor or praise, is evident in this word.

consummation (kahn suh MAY sh'n), the act of consummating, or the state of being consummated; completion; fulfillment: *The trip abroad was the consummation of his long-held desires*.

consummately (kun SUM m't lee), in consummate manner: *She was consummately happy with the recognition of her work*.

contiguous (kun TIG yoo 's) Touching, in direct contact: *She wanted the tiles in a contiguous arrangement;* near without actually touching, although this is not as common. In the second sense, it is synonymous with adjacent, which means neighboring, nearby, but not necessarily touching: *The playground was contiguous to the school, beyond the tennis courts*.

contiguously (kun TIG yoo 's lee), in a contiguous fashion: *She lined up the boxes contiguously on the shelf*.

contiguity (kahn tuh GYOO uh tee), the state of being contiguous; intimate association, nearness: *The contiguity of the two families caused some strain in relations*. Also, **contiguousness** (kun TIG yoo 's n's).

correlation (kawr uh LAY sh'n; kahr uh LAY sh'n) The mutual relation of two or more things or parts: *Tests seem to demonstrate that there is a high correlation between language aptitudes and intelligence;* or the act of placing or bringing into a mutual relation: *He was engaged in the correlation of two sets of figures, hoping to discover the basis for a predictable trend;* or the state of being brought into such a relation.

correlate (KAWR uh late; KAHR uh late), the verb, means to bring into correlation, establish in orderly connection: *Many schools now try to correlate the teaching of subjects in the humanities.*

As a noun it means either of two related things, especially when one implies the other: *Speed in typing is a correlate of manual skill.*

correlative (kuh REL uh tive), so related that each implies or complements the other; mutually related: *"Either" and "or" are correlative words.*

As a noun, it refers to either of two things which are mutually related; it may be used as a synonym for correlate.

culminate (KUL muh nate) To reach the highest point, the summit, or highest development. It is usually followed by *in: Her years of vocal study culminated in an opera debut which drew the highest critical praise.* It is not uncommon now to hear culminate used as a synonym for terminate, without reference to success or good, as in saying: *one's efforts culminated in failure.*

   culmination (kul muh NAY sh'n), the highest point, consummation; that in which anything culminates: *Her opera debut represented the culmination of years of study;* or the act or fact of culmination.

cumulative (KYOO muh lay t'v) This word and its derivatives have their origin in the Latin *cumulus,* a heap. This adjective means formed by or increased by successive additions: *The cumulative weight of the various bits of evidence left little doubt as to where the guilt lay.*

   cumulate (KYOO myuh late) is a less common form of the verb *accumulate,* to collect, gather into a mass.

   cumulation (kyoo myuh LAY sh'n), a heap or mass; or the act of forming or collecting one.

   cumulatively (KYOO myuh lay t'v lee), in a cumulative fashion.

   cumulativeness (KYOO myuh lay t'v n's), the disposition to be cumulative: *Her cumulativeness over the years had filled the attic with books and old furniture.*

debility (duh BIL uh tee) Weakness, especially in a physical sense; state of being feeble: *His long illness resulted in a debility which kept him confined to a wheelchair.*

   debilitate (duh BIL uh tate), to weaken or enfeeble. The verb is more often used in a figurative sense than the noun: *An unfortunate investment debilitated his resources.*

   debilitated (duh BIL uh tay t'd), weakened, or impaired vitality: *her debilitated condition after the long journey.*

   debilitation (duh bil uh TAY sh'n) also means weakness, but has more the sense of the process or the act of debilitating than debility: *the debilitation of the family fortunes.*

debonair (deb uh NAIR) Of pleasant manners, courteous, especially in a gay or light-hearted manner. This is from the Old French phrase, *de bon aire*, of good disposition: *His debonair ways were particularly attractive to her in contrast to John's stuffiness*.

debonairly (deb uh NAIR lee), in agreeable, jaunty fashion.

debonairness (deb uh NAIR n's) is the noun signifying the manner itself, or the possession of it.

decadent (duh KAY d'nt; DEK uh d'nt) Falling off or deteriorating, usually applied to social conditions or intellectual, spiritual, or aesthetic qualities: *A decadent trend had been apparent in the neighborhood for the past few years, causing many families with young children to move out*. As a noun, the word refers specifically to a member of a group of predominantly French writers and artists at the end of the nineteenth century whose work emphasized a highly refined, subtle style and explored artificial, abnormal, eccentric, or morbid subjects. From this association, decadent as applied to art has a particularly strong negative tone. Also, **decadency**.

decadence (duh KAY d'ns; DEK uh d'ns), the act or process of falling into an inferior condition; decay; deterioration: *Corruption and irresponsibility of public officials are signs of the decadence of a society. His public utterances showed a moral decadence which shocked those who had been out of touch with him*. The noun also refers to the artistic movement of the decadents and its spirit.

decadently (duh KAY d'nt lee; DEK uh d'nt lee), in a manner falling away from a condition of goodness or excellence.

The relation to *decay* in all these words is obvious. The source is the Latin *cadere*, to fall, also the source of cadence. But the *de-* as prefix gives an especially strong sense of falling or going down from something.

decorum (duh KAWR 'm) Appropriateness of behavior, speech, dress, etc.: *Her decorum on being presented to her mother-in-law's friends left nothing to be desired;* a standard of what is proper and fitting in polite society: *The decorum of the meeting was shattered by a series of interruptions from members of the audience not recognized by the chairman*. Also, **decorousness**.

decorous (DEK uh r's; duh KAWR 's), characterized by propriety in conduct, manners, appearance, character, etc.

decorously (DEC uh r's lee; duh KAWR's lee), in a seemly, dignified fashion: *She decorously accepted his gift, expressing her thanks in a quiet, formal manner*.

Decorum, propriety, and *etiquette* all imply observance of the formal requirements of society governing behavior. *Decorum* suggests dignity and a sense of what is becoming: *propriety,* conformance to established conventions of morals and good taste, with emphasis on adherence to the rules rather than an innate sense of what is appropriate: *etiquette,* a body of conventional forms and usage.

decrepit (duh KREP 't) Broken down or weakened by old age: feeble, infirm: *Leaning on his cane as he shuffled along, he looked too decrepit to be able to reach the end of the block.* The Latin source is a verb meaning to creak or rattle, suggesting that the derivation is from the creakiness of the bones of a decrepit person.

decrepitude (duh KREP uh tood; duh KREP uh tyood), weakened condition; feebleness, especially from old age: *The colonial house was in a state of decrepitude.*

decrepitly (deh KREP 't lee), in a decrepit manner.

There is a distinction between *decrepit* and several other words of similiar meaning. *Decrepit, weak,* and *feeble* are similar in meaning, but *decrepit* implies being old and broken in health to a marked degree. *Weak* is simply not strong. *Feeble* applies more to a kind of worn down weakness and frailty.

delectable (duh LEK tuh b'l) This means highly pleasing or enjoyable: *The food was as delectable to the taste as it was appealing to the eye.*

delectably (duh LEK tuh blee), in a pleasing manner: *The fruits were delectably displayed.*

delectability (duh lek tuh BIL uh tee), state or quality of being delectable. Also, **delectableness** (duh LEK tuh b'l n's).

Delectable, delicious, and *delightful* all describe something which gives pleasure. *Delicious* means affording pleasure to the senses, especially those of taste and smell. The first two words carry a sense of refined enjoyment. *Delightful* also means extremely pleasing, but has a broader area of association than that of the senses: *It was a delightful experience to meet such a charming person.*

deleterious (del uh TEER y's) Harmful, injurious: *deleterious influences;* destructive, harmful to health: *She was convinced his irregular eating and sleeping habits would prove deleterious.*

deleteriously (del uh TEER y's lee), in a harmful or destructive manner: *His long stay in tropical climates affected him deleteriously.*

deleteriousness (del uh TEER y's n's), state or quality of being harmful.

demagogue (DEM uh gawg; DEM uh gahg) Originally meaning a leader of the people, this word has lost stature in modern times. It now refers to a leader who uses the passions and prejudices of the people to further his own interests: *Skillful in touching the emotions of the crowd, a demagogue is most likely to appear in times of instability and dissatisfaction, when people are looking for leadership in new quarters.*

demagoguery (DEM uh gawg uh ree; DEM uh gahg uh ree), the methods or practices of a demagogue; or having the character of a demagogue: *Even his sponsors found his demagoguery offensive.* Also, **demagogism.**

demagogic (dem uh GAHJ ik; dem uh GAGH ik), pertaining to or characteristic of a demagogue: *His audience was too sophisticated for such demagogic tactics as his flag-waving patriotism and hysterical accusations.* Also, **demagogical.**

deprecate (DEP ruh kate) To express earnest disapproval of; to protest; to urge reasons against: *He deprecated her impulsive furthering of every cause that came along.*

deprecation (dep ruh KAY sh'n), expression of disapproval or protest: *His deprecation of the project discouraged the others.*

deprecatory (DEP ruh kuh tawr ee), expressing deprecation, of a deprecating nature: *His deprecatory remarks about his own work were intended to convey modesty.* Also, **deprecative.**

deprecatingly (DEP ruh kay ting lee), in a deprecating manner.

Deprecate is often confused with *depreciate,* to lessen the value of, to represent as of little value, to belittle: *He was warned not to depreciate the abilities of others in comparison with his own. The property kept depreciating in value.*

desecration (des uh KRAY sh'n) As *consecration* means dedication to a high or holy purpose or office, desecration means the turning of a person, object, or office from a sacred to a profane purpose; violation of sanctity: *It would have been a desecration of the priesthood for him to abandon those who depended on him for spiritual guidance;* or the condition of anything so treated: *The desecration that met her eyes in the little chapel moved her to tears.* Although the word strictly refers to sacred things, it has also come to be used in a more general sense for violation or abuse: *desecration of the land by improper use; desecration of the truth*.

desecrate (DES uh krate), to treat with sacrilege, to divert from a sacred to a profane purpose.

desecrater, desecrator (DES uh kray t'r), one who commits an act of desecration.

deviate (DEE vee ate) This word comes from the Latin phrase *de via*, from the way, and means to turn aside; to depart from a course of action or line of thought: *No argument could persuade him to deviate from his intention to make the journey*.

As a noun it is pronounced differently (DEE vee 't), and in psychological terminology, it means an individual who strikingly departs from the average in any respect.

deviation (dee vee AY sh'n), the act of deviating; variation from the common way: *His continual deviation from the rules was not intentional, but it was a disturbing factor to the others*.

deviant (DEE vee 'nt), an adjective, means tending to deviate.

deviator (DEE vee ay t'r) is one who deviates.

Deviate, digress, diverge, and *swerve* all imply turning or going aside from a path. To *deviate* is to turn or wander slightly from the most direct or desirable way to an end. One can *deviate* physically, morally, or intellectually. *Digress* has more the idea of wandering from the main subject in speaking or writing, especially by way of explanation. *Diverge* implies a separation of one course into two, at some point from which they move increasingly farther apart. To *swerve* is to make a sudden sharp turn from a path, often to return to it; it refers more to physical action.

dexterity (dek STAIR uh tee) Ease or expertness in using the hands or the body: *To play the piano well requires great manual dexterity;* and by extension, although this sense is not as commonly used, quickness and skill in controlling mental powers: *His dexterity in mathematical calculation astonished his teachers*. Also, **dexterousness**.

dexterous, dextrous (DEX ster 's; DEK str's), skillful; expert in physical movements; clever. The word also means right-handed (from Latin *dexter*, right). It is rarely used in this sense, although it appears in *ambidextrous*, meaning equally adept with both hands.

dexterously, dextrously (DEK ster 's lee; DEK str's lee), skillfully.

dilemma (dih LEM uh) A situation requiring a choice between equally undesirable alternatives; an embarrassing situation: *She found herself in the dilemma of having to offend her hostess by refusing the invitation or submitting to a weekend of utter boredom.*

Dilemma, predicament, plight, and *quandary* are all uncomfortable positions to be in. *Dilemma* presents an element of puzzlement which is also present in *predicament,* but the latter is more likely to be unpleasant, trying, or dangerous. *Plight,* which originally meant peril, is now synonymous with predicament. It is a rather high-flown word, used in formal writing, but most often used humorously: *He was in the plight of a man with an itching nose and an armful of packages.* A *quandary* is the state of perplexity of one facing a difficult situation: *She was in a quandary about whether to sell the house.*

discretion (dis KRESH 'n) The right of deciding or acting according to one's own free judgment or choice: *He was told he would be given discretion to deal with any opposition from within the ranks;* the quality of being careful or discriminating as to what is necessary or desirable, particularly in regard to one's own behavior: *The difficult task of shifting the personnel so that everyone was satisfied was accomplished with admirable discretion on her part.* This latter sense implies cautiousness and reserve, a desire to prevent embarrassment.

discretionary (dis KRESH 'n air ee), subject or left to one's discretion, pertaining to discretion: *the discretionary powers of the president.*

discreet (dis KREET), is a related adjective meaning wise or careful in avoiding mistakes or faults; cautious, reserved, not rash: *He is very discreet in his choice of friends.*

dissimulate (dih SIM yuh late) To disguise or conceal under a false appearance, to pretend to be other than what one is: *His attempt to dissumulate about his financial state was pathetic to those who knew the truth.*

dissumulation (dih sim yuh LAY sh'n), act of pretending, hypocrisy: *The role she assumed of a gracious generous lady was pure dissimulation.*

dissimulator (dih SIM yuh lay t'r), one who practices dissimulation.

Dissimulate and *simulate* both come from the same Latin word, *similis,* meaning like, but simulate does not have such a strong suggestion of intent to deceive. It may mean to pretend, or to assume a false appearance: *to simulate illness;* or it may mean merely to imitate: *She tried to simulate the style of her teacher in her own performance.*

docile (DAH s'l) This is from the Latin adjective derived from *docere,* to teach. It means readily taught or trained. The more common sense of manageable or gentle is a development from the first: *Teachers of young children usually find girls more docile than boys.*

    docilely (DAH suh lee), in docile fashion: *She followed docilely, as instructed.*

    docility (dah SIL uh tee; do SIL uh tee), willingness to be taught, manageability: *The docility of the prisoners was undoubtedly due to fear of punishment.*

    All these words suggest lack of will, no resistance.

dogmatic (dawg MAAT ik) The most frequent use pertains to asserting opinions in an authoritative, arrogant, or positive manner: *The dogmatic way in which he expressed his views made it impossible to have a real exchange of opinion.* This meaning developed from a more specific one, pertaining to a system of principles, as those of a church. A dogma is a set of beliefs or a principle which is held as settled opinion. It is based on assumptions rather than proof: *The dogma of his political party was that governmental interference must be held to a minimum under all conditions.*

    dogmatically (dawg MAAT uh k'lee), in a dogmatic manner: *He asserted dogmatically that his country was best.*

    dogmatism (DAWG muh tizm), positive, arrogant assertion of opinions, or dogmatic character: *He could make no headway in his reforms against the dogmatism of the elders.*

    dogmatize (DAWG muh tize), to make dogmatic assertions.

    dogmatist (DAWG muh tist), one who asserts positively his own opinions; one who lays down dogma.

eccentric (ek SEN trik) Deviating from the usual character or practice; irregular; peculiar. As an adjective, the word may apply to a person, a course, or behavior: *Even in his youth he had been eccentric, often dropping out of sight without explanation for days at a time. He had eccentric ways, eccentric enthusiasms.*

    As a noun, it refers to an unusual, odd, or peculiar person: *Because of his miserly habits and odd appearance, he developed a reputation as an eccentric.* The core of the word is *center.* Thus the literal meaning, in mathematics, is not having the same center. The application to people and things has developed from that.

eccentrically (ek SEN truh k'lee), in an erratic or peculiar manner.

eccentricity (ek sen TRIS uh tee), an oddity or peculiarity: *It is his eccentricity never to accept a dinner invitation;* or the quality of being eccentric: *The eccentricity of the weather spoiled all their plans.*

efficacious (ef uh KAY sh's) Capable of achieving a certain result, often demonstrated only when actually employed: *He determined by trial and error which method was the most efficacious.*

efficaciously (ef uh KAY sh's lee), in an efficacious manner.

efficaciousness (ef uh KAY sh's n's), state or quality of being efficacious.

efficacy (EF uh kuh see), capacity for serving to produce effects: *The efficacy of the remedy was demonstrated by his quick recovery.*

Efficacious must be distinguished from *effective, effectual,* and *efficient.* Effective is applied to that which has power to or actually does produce a desired effect: *His speech was effective in recruiting volunteers.* This word has a particular American usage in application to a law: *it is effective when it becomes operative.* If it accomplishes its purpose, it is *effectual,* a word of praise applied to that which produces the desired effect: *an effectual way to silence him.* Efficient means the same thing, with the added suggestion of achieving results by skillful use of energy and a minimum of wasted effort. This is applied to people as well as action: *an efficient group of workers; an efficient plan of action.*

egregious (ih GREE jus) This adjective comes from a Latin word meaning out of the flock, not one of the herd, hence outstanding. Formerly it had favorable overtones: *egregious virtues; egregious talents.* But today its use is restricted to unfavorable judgments and carries (perhaps from its continual use in reference to an untruth) a strong note of contempt. It now means glaring, notorious, or scandalous: *He is an egregious fool.*

egregiously (ih GREE jus lee), in an egregious manner.

egregiousness (ih GREE jus n's), the quality of being egregious.

eloquent (EL uh kw'nt) Having or using the power of fluent, appropriate expression: *He was eloquent in his criticism of the* *proposed measure;* characterized by such expression: *It was an eloquent criticism he gave;* movingly expressive: *The music was an eloquent expression of mood.*

eloquently (EL uh kw'nt lee), in a fluent, expressive manner.

eloquence (EL uh kw'ns), the action or art of using language with fluency, power, and aptness; or eloquent language in speaking or writing.

elusive (ih LOO s'v) Not easily grasped or understood, as ideas or qualities: *Some of the new mathematical theories were too elusive for him, handicapped as he was by lack of recent study;* hard to express or define: *Her elusive charm, though many felt it, defied analysis;* evasive: *The elusive couple managed to stay in hiding until their pursuers gave up.*

elude (ih LOOD), the verb form, to escape or avoid by cleverness, to slip away from: *He eluded the waiting reporters by using the side exit;* to baffle; to escape the mind: *The reason for her sudden decision eludes me.*

elusiveness (ih LOO s'v n's), the quality of being elusive: *the essential elusiveness of the subject;* or the state of being so: *His consistent elusiveness discouraged the friends who kept trying to see him.*

elusively (ih LOO s'v lee), evasively; in a manner not easily understood.

Elusive, illusive, and *allusive* are easily confused, particularly in speaking. *Elusive* and *illusive* are pronounced in the same way. There is also a certain apparent relation in the meaning of *illusive* as deceptive, which is somewhat similar to the idea of *elusive* as evasive, avoiding by cleverness. But *illusive* has to do with something unreal, or false: *She gave an illusive impression of height for a small woman;* while the central idea of *elusive* is escape or avoidance.

Allusive, also with similar pronunciation, means having incidental reference to something not fully expressed, or characterized by such references: *His books were so allusive to the works of obscure writers that only scholars had the knowledge to appreciate them fully.*

emanate (EM uh nate) To flow out or proceed, as from a source or origin, with the suggestion of spreading or streaming; used of nonmaterial things: *The heat emanating from the fireplace warmed even the corners of the room. Love emanated from God.*

emanation (em uh NAY sh'n), act of emanating: *The steady emanation of light from the house in the distance encouraged them to keep on;* something that emanates.

emanative (EM uh nay t'v), that which emanates or flows out of.

emulate (EM yuh late) To imitate with an effort to equal or excel; it implies a standard to be reached: *The writer he hoped to emulate was Hemingway;* or to rival with some degree of success: *Fans of Roger Maris agreed that he successfully emulated Babe Ruth.*

emulation (em yuh LAY sh'n), effort or desire to equal or excel others; rivalry: *He strenuously applied himself to the emulation of a series of notably successful men.*

emulative (EM yuh lay t'v), characterized by or tending to emulation: *an emulative desire to do as well as his older brother.*

emulatively (EM yuh lay t'v lee), in an emulative manner: *He responded emulatively to the tales of great men which his parents told him.*

emulator (EM yuh lay t'r), one who emulates.

emulous (EM yuh l's), desirous of equaling or excelling. This word is not commonly used.

enervate (EN 'r vate) To deprive of nervous strength; weaken; destroy the vigor of: *As he grew older he found that it enervated him to take long trips.*

enervation (en 'r VAY sh'n), state of weakness: *The enervation she always felt in summer was something she dreaded to look forward to;* the process of weakening: *A steady enervation was apparent in his condition, despite all the treatments and remedies the doctors tried.*

Because of the first two syllables, *enervate* is often thought to be related to *energy,* with a meaning similar to *invigorate.* This is exactly the opposite of its true meaning. The core of *enervate* is from *nerve,* and the association is a negative one, *without* nervous strength. Its antonym is *innervate,* meaning to stimulate.

enigma (uh NIG muh) Something puzzling or unexplainable, like a riddle or obscure saying: *Struggle as he would to understand them, James Joyce's later works remained an enigma to him.* Sometimes a person difficult to understand, or one whose feelings are hard to penetrate, is called an enigma.

Enigma, puzzle, and *riddle* all refer to something baffling or confusing which is to be solved. *Enigma* suggests an element of mysteriousness. *Puzzle* refers to a question perplexing to the mind, sometimes contrived to test one's mental abilities. A *riddle* is an intentionally obscure statement or question, whose meaning or answer can only be arrived at by guessing.

enigmatic (en ig MAAT ik), perplexing, mysterious: *The circumstances were very enigmatic and did not seem to fit together*.

enigmatically (en ig MAAT uh k'lee), in a perplexing or mysterious manner.

erudition (air yuh DISH 'n) Acquired knowledge, especially in literature, languages, and history, etc., as distinguished from the sciences; scholarship: *His erudition in Oriental history and the stimulating way in which he communicated it were an inspiration to generations of students*. Also, **eruditeness** (AIR yuh dite n's).

erudite (AIR yuh dite), learned or scholarly: *an erudite exposition of the subject*.

eruditely (AIR yuh dite lee), in an erudite manner.

Erudition suggests a thorough and profound formal knowledge obtained by extensive research. *Learning* is knowledge acquired by systematic study in an academic field, but with a suggestion of less depth and comprehensiveness than *erudition*. Both words refer to knowledge gained by study rather than experience.

exonerate (eg ZAHN uh rate) The *-oner-* is from the Latin *onus*, load or burden (the English word *onus* has the same meaning). To exonerate someone is to free him of a burden or charge, thus clear him of blame, or relieve him of an obligation or duty: *He was exonerated of all blame when the guilty person came forward. The judge exonerated him from paying a penalty*.

exoneration (eg zahn uh RAY sh'n), the act of freeing from obligation or blame: *The public exoneration restored his stature in the community;* the state of being so freed.

exonerative (eg ZAHN uh ruh t'v), freeing from a burden or obligation: *an exonerative judgement by the committee*.

extenuate (ek STEN yoo ate) From the Latin meaning to make thin, this word has come to mean to make less of, with particular application to faults; to make bad behavior seem better, or less serious, by finding excuses: *A penalty for wrongdoing is sometimes lightened if there are extenuating circumstances. I cannot extenuate his rude behavior to my sister*.

extenuation (ek sten yoo AY sh'n), the act of extenuating: *The judge agreed that his feeble-mindedness was an extenuation of the crime;* the state of being extenuated; a partial excuse: *the only extenuation I have to offer for forgetting*.

extenuative (ek STEN yoo ay t'v), that which extenuates, extenuating.

extenuatively (ek STEN yoo uh t'v lee), in extenuation.

extenuatory (ek STEN yoo uh tawr ee), tending to extenuate: *He might consider those facts extenuatory if you called them to his attention.*

extraneous (eks TRAY nee 's) The *extra-* conveys the sense of outside or beyond; the whole word means introduced from the outside; not belonging to or proper to a thing; foreign: *If we are not careful to exclude extraneous issues, the meeting will go on forever. Extraneous matter in his eye caused discomfort.*

extraneously (eks TRAY nee 's lee)

extraneousness (eks TRAY nee 's n's), irrelevance; state of being extraneous: *The extraneousness of his remarks revealed that he had not been paying attention.*

facilitate (fuh SIL uh tate) The source of this word is the Latin *facilis*, easy (also related to *facile* and *facility*). It means simply to make easy or help forward: *Proper equipment would facilitate an earlier completion of this project;* or to assist someone's progress: *He was the kind of person who enjoyed facilitating the careers of promising young men.*

facilitation (fuh sil uh TAY sh'n), the act or process of facilitating: *The facilitation of transportation was partly responsible for the population increase in the area.*

facility (fuh SIL uh tee), means something that makes any action easier: *The wheel provided man with the facility for moving objects over land.* It carries with it the sense of ease and dexterity: *He had developed great facility in typing by the time he finished the course.*

fallacy (FAAL uh see) A misleading or false notion: *Many old superstitions are still believed, even though they have long since been proved to be fallacies;* a deceptive or unsound argument: *His opponent demonstrated the fallacy in his position by proving that the figures he used no longer applied.*

fallacious (fuh LAY sh's), deceptive, misleading: *His fallacious account made his listeners think that he had been the hero of the skirmish instead of the deserter he actually was;* logically unsound: *His fallacious reasoning led him to an embarrasingly mistaken conclusion.*

fallaciousness (fuh LAY sh's n's), falseness, unsoundness.

fallaciously (fuh LAY sh's lee), in a deceptive or unsound manner.

fatuous (FAACH OO 's) Foolish, especially in an unconscious, self-satisfied way: *The fatuous commonplaces, which he regarded as wisdom and uttered with solemn gravity, made him a laughingstock.* Fatuous is a slightly changed form of the Latin *fatuus,* foolish.

    fatuitous (fuh TYOO uh t's), characterized by complacent folly.

    fatuity (fuh TYOO uh tee), foolish, complacent stupidity.

    fatuously (FAACH OO 's lee), foolishly, in a pompous, self-satisfied way.

    fatuousness (FAACH OO 's n's), bland, self-satisfied foolishness.

    infatuated (in FAACH OO ay t'd), to have been made foolish, especially by an excess of love: *She is infatuated with him, but he doesn't care a bit for her.*

    Ignis fatuus is a Medieval Latin phrase meaning "fool's fire." It was applied to phosphorescent lights over marshes—also called will-o-the-wisp—which misled night wanderers. Today *ignis fatuus* is used chiefly to suggest dangerously misleading ideas or alluring errors: *Speculation about a rift between Russia and Poland may be an ignis fatuus.*

feasible (FEE zuh b'l) Capable of being done: *Considering the resources, the plan seems feasible enough;* suitable: *A location at this intersection is especially feasible for a service station.*

    feasibility (fee zuh BIL uh tee), quality of being feasible, practicability: *The lack of feasibility of her projects never seemed to dampen her enthusiasm.* Also, **feasibleness** (FEE zuh b'l n's).

    feasibly (FEE zuh blee), in a feasible manner: *It could be feasibly arranged.*

    In one sense, *feasible* means *possible,* but they cannot always be used interchangeably. What is *possible* is able to be done and often likely, but *feasible* suggests the ease with which something can be done and its suitability: *Last year a trip to Europe seemed barely possible, but this year it is feasible.*

fervent (FER v'nt) From the Latin word meaning to burn or glow; this means having or showing great warmth or intensity of feeling: *Her fervent admiration of her teacher was so obvious that it was embarrasing to him.*

    fervency (FER v'n see), warmth of feeling, ardor: *the fervency of her appeal for mercy for her son.*

    fervently (FER v'nt lee), in a warm, intense manner: *She prayed fervently for his success.*

    fervor (FER v'r), warmth; intensity.

Fervid (from the same source) is even more intense than *fervent* suggesting a feverish, overheated kind of enthusiasm. *Ardent* is similar in meaning also, but implies an eager devotion to a person or cause: *an ardent lover*.

figment (fig m'nt) A product of the imagination; a pure invention; a made-up story, often designed to explain, justify, or glorify oneself: *All the stories he had told about his associations with theatrical people turned out to be pure figment. A figment of your imagination can lead to delusion*.

    figmental (fig MEN t'l)

Fiction, which comes from the same source word meaning to shape, to make up, is also a product of the imagination, and may have the same suggestion of deceit: *He almost came to believe in the fiction he had circulated about his being a romantic war hero*. But more often it is imaginative invention designed to entertain, as in prose literature: *Light fiction was all she could absorb after a long day's work*.

flagrant (flAY gr'nt) From the Latin meaning burning. This word means glaringly—that is, flamingly—obvious. The implication is unfavorable: scandalous, outrageous, notorious: *The flagrant manner in which she followed him all over the country subjected her to universal criticism. In flagrante delicto* means literally while the crime is blazing, thus in the very act.

    flagrancy (flAY gr'n see), condition or quality of being flagrant, outrageousness: *The flagrancy of the crime shocked even the police*. Also, **flagrance.**

    flagrantly (flAY gr'nt lee), in a glaring manner: *He flagrantly ignored the needs of those dependent on him*.

flamboyant (flaam BOY 'nt) This word was originally applied to the shape of flames. It is still used in architecture as a technical term for the wavy flamelike appearance of Gothic ornamental stonework. Then it came to suggest the color of flames. From this the idea of gorgeousness, then showiness, developed. Except as applied to color itself, in nature or in paintings, the word suggests gaudiness or poor taste: *His flamboyant style of dress marked him as an exhibitionist*.

    flamboyantly (flaam BOY 'nt lee), in flamboyant style or manner.

    flamboyance (flaam BOY 'ns), ornateness, showiness. Also, **flamboyancy** (flaam BOY 'n see).

garrulous (GAAR uh l's; GAAR yuh l's) Given to much talk, especially about trifles; wordy: *She put off visiting her garrulous old aunt until she knew she would have enough time to listen to the usual long reminiscences.*

garrulously (GAAR uh l's lee; GAAR yul l's lee), in garrulous fashion.

garrulity (guh ROO luh tee), disposition to talk tiresomely about trifles. Also, **garrulousness** (GAAR uh l's n's; GAAR yuh l's n's).

Garrulous, talkative, and *loquacious* all refer to one who talks a great deal. A *garrulous* person prattles on, especially about trifles; a *talkative* one talks a great deal; a *loquacious* one has a constant flow of language, usually with intent to be sociable.

geniality (jee nee AAL uh tee) Sympathetic cheerfulness or kindliness; warmth of disposition; cordiality: *His geniality made him a favorite host and welcome guest, as he always managed to create an atmosphere of easy friendliness.*

genial (JEEN y'l), sympathetically cheerful: *His unfailingly genial disposition was a great asset in campaigning;* or enlivening, pleasantly warm, or mild: *The genial climate of Florida attracted them every winter.*

genially (JEEN yuh lee), in warm sympathetic manner.

Congeniality (kun jee nee AAL uh tee), meaning likeness of mind, taste, or disposition, often has the same suggestion of warmth and good feeling as *geniality,* since in one sense it is a sharing of geniality: *The congeniality of the gathering prompted them to plan regular reunions.* But it does not necessarily always have pleasant overtones: *Since they had both recently become widowers, they found a certain melancholy congeniality in each other's company.*

gregarious (gruh GAIR ee 's) This word is derived from one meaning herd. Gregarious people flock together, like to be in groups, are sociable, fond of company: *His gregarious disposition sometimes led him into unsuitable company.* It also means pertaining to a flock or crowd.

gregariously (gruh GAIR y's lee), in gregarious fashion.

gregariousness (gruh GAIR y's n's), disposition to move in a herd, or to seek the society of others: *Her husband's gregariousness kept their social calendar filled.*

grotesque (gro TESK) Specifically this applies to a strange, often ugly style of decorative art of a fantastic nature in which human, animal, and plant forms are shaped and combined in unlikely ways. From this, the word has come to mean odd or unnatural in appearance or character; fantastically ugly or absurd; bizarre: *Sideshow freaks trade on their grotesque appearance or abilities. That African mask is grotesque.*

As a noun the word means any strange, absurd object or person.

grotesquely (gro TESK lee), in a fantastic or absurd manner.

grotesqueness (gro TESK n's), strangeness, grotesque character or nature.

grotesquery (gro TESK uh ree), something grotesque; grotesque character: *The grotesquery of the predicament almost made him laugh, painful as it was;* or grotesque work: *The gargoyles on Notre Dame cathedral in Paris are a famous example of grotesquery.*

hallucination (huh loo sih NAY sh'n) Perception of objects or experience of sensation for which there is no real external cause; illusion: *She suffered a succession of frightening hallucinations, always when she was alone, and at twilight. His appearance was so sudden and quiet she almost believed it was a hallucination.* The word comes from the Greek, to wander in mind, hence the suggestion of the imperfect functioning of faculties.

hallucinate (huh LOO sih nate), to have a hallucination of; to have hallucinations: *They could always tell when she was hallucinating by the strange expression in her eyes.*

hallucinatory (huh LOO sih nuh tawr ee), pertaining to or characterized by hallucination: *her hallucinatory notions.*

Hallucination, illusion, and *delusion* all refer to various kinds of mental deceptions.

A *hallucination* is a completely groundless perception caused by a disordered imagination; it applies to a pathological condition. An *illusion* may be a false interpretation of something real: *On the stage, the cheap satin created the illusion of richness,* as well as something imagined. A *delusion* is an unshakable mistaken idea, often harmful or troublesome, about something which really exists: *He had the delusion that he was irresistible to all women.*

harass (HAAR 's; huh RAAS) To disturb persistently; torment with troubles and cares: *He was so harassed by requests for appearances at benefits, contributions, and interviews that his fame became a burden.* In a military sense, it refers to repeated raids or attacks: *Since they knew the enemy was weak, their plan was to harass them until they surrendered.*

harassment (HAAR 's m'nt), act of harassing, or state of being harassed: *The harassment by his creditors finally drove him to leave town;* worry or annoyance: *The harassment of telephone calls at all hours of the night was beginning to tell on her nerves.*

harassingly (HAAR 's ing lee), in a harassing way.

harasser (HAAR 's 'r), tormentor, one who harasses. *Harass* and *harry* both indicate trouble by repeated attacks. But to *harry* is to persecute by unreasonable demands or constant ill-treatment: *He harried his blackmail victim into a state of nervous collapse.* In terms of war, it is to invade, rob, and lay waste: *The guerrilla band harried the village and seized the food supplies.* It is stronger than *harass,* which refers more to bothersome annoyances.

hazardous (HAAZ 'r d's) Dangerous; risky: *Even for the experienced, mountain climbing is one of the most hazardous of sports;* dependent on chance: *Hazardous as the undertaking looked, he felt the possibility of great success justified it.* The source of this word is the Arabic *az-zahr,* the die. Hazard was an old game of chance played with dice, hence the connotation of risk.

hazardously (HAAZ 'r d's lee), in a manner exposing oneself to danger or chance: *He teetered hazardously on the brink.*

hazardousness (HAAZ 'r d's n's), danger, chanciness.

hazard (HAAZ 'rd) as a noun means exposure to danger or harm: *The pioneers suffered untold hazards on their journeys westward.* As a verb it means to expose to risk; to venture: *He timidly hazarded an opinion which was rudely laughed down.*

hierarchy (HEYE uh rahr kee) A system of persons or things in a graded order: *As a brilliant young prospect in the organization, he had worked his way through the lower steps of the hierarchy in short order.* "Going through channels" is a popular way of expressing the procedure of going through the levels of a hierarchy in orderly fashion to convey a communication or get something done. The word originally referred—and still does in a more specific sense—to the body of church officials in successive ranks or orders. This meaning derived from the idea of a rank of angels. Hierarchy also means dominion or authority in sacred things: *The hierarchy of the church in certain matters is indisputable.*

hierarchical (heye uh RAHR k' k'l), of or belonging to a hierarchy: *a hierarchical social structure, such as the caste system.*

hierarch (HEYE uh rahrk), one who rules or has authority in sacred things: from the Greek, meaning sacred leader.

homogeneous (ho muh JEE nee 's) Composed of parts all of the same kind; of the same kind or nature: *It was an unusually homogeneous community; the great majority of the residents were of the same social and economic class, with similar educational patterns and cultural background.* The Greek source is *homos*, the same, and *genos*, kind.

homogeneity (ho muh juh NEE uh tee), composition of parts of the same kind: *homogeneity of a substance; homogeneity of a group.* Also, **homogeneousness.**

homogeneously (ho muh JEE nee 's lee), in homogeneous manner.

Homogeneous must be distinguished from *homogenous* (huh MAHJ uh n's), which is a biological term obviously related to it. *Homogenous* corresponds in structure because of a common origin. We hear it more commonly in the verb form, *homogenize*, (huh MAHJ uh nize), to make substances homogeneous by breaking them down and blending their components.

The opposite of *homogeneous* is *heterogeneous*, of different kinds; *heteros* means other or different.

hypochondria (heye puh KAHN dree uh) Depressed spirits caused by worry over imaginary ailments: *Physical causes having been ruled out by the medical tests, her father could only conclude she was suffering from hypochondria, and began thinking of other ways to deal with her abnormal worry.* The Greek word referred to the parts of the body under the cartilage of the breastbone, once thought to be the seat of melancholy.

hypochondriac (heye puh KAHN dree aak), one suffering from or subject to hypochondria.

As an adjective it means suffering from hypochondria. Also, **hypochondriacal** (heye puh kun DRI uh k'l).

hypochondriacally (heye puh kun DRI uh k'lee), in a hypochondriacal manner.

hypothetical (heye puh THET uh k'l) Assumed for purposes of argument or investigation; supposed: *The hypothetical circumstances he described sounded so familiar that I suspected him of trying to trap me;* or pertaining to such assumption: *a hypothetical approach; hypothetical reason.* Hypothetical is often used as the opposite of practical, of something that actually works or can be put into practice.

hypothetically (heye puh THET uh k'lee), in hypothetical manner; from hypothetical viewpoint: *Hypothetically the plan should have worked.*

hypothesis (heye POTH uh sis) is the noun from which hypothetical is derived. It is a proposition or principle proposed to explain an apparently related group of occurrences or things; a guide to investigation in the light of established facts. It is, however, an assumption for working purposes, not itself demonstrated as true. *A theory* similarly is a principle of explanation not conclusively proven. But a theory has more standing, as a more or less verified or established explanation, as the *theory of relativity.*

hypothetic (heye puh THET ik)

hypothesize (heye PAHTH uh size), to form a hypothesis, or to assume by hypothesis: *He hypothesized a beginning registration of 200.*

ideology (eye dee AHL uh jee; id ee AHL uh jee) The usage of this word has been extended from the science of ideas to the system of beliefs, ideas, and symbols of a social movement, institution, class, or large group. It may refer even more specifically to some political or social beliefs or system, along with the devices for putting them into operation: *The children in any society are taught the prevailing ideology directly and indirectly from babyhood on.* It also means theorizing of a visionary or unpractical nature: *He has some vague ideology embodying an ideal society.*

ideologic (eye dee uh LAHJ ik; id ee uh LAHJ ik), pertaining to ideology; visionary; of the nature of impractical theorizing. Also, **ideological.**

ideologist (eye dee AHL uh jist; id ee AHL uh jist) one who deals with a system of ideas, an expert in ideology; it has a narrower reference than ideology. Although it may also mean a visionary, it is rarely heard in this sense.

idiosyncrasy (id ee uh SIN kruh see) A characteristic, physical or mental (but usually applying to behavior or belief), peculiar to an individual: *It was an idiosyncrasy of his never to read a book on the best-seller list.*

idiosyncratic (id ee uh sin KRAAT ik), peculiar to an individual; of peculiar temper or inclination: *His idiosyncratic notions made him a difficult, crotchety companion.*

Idiosyncrasy is somewhat similar to *eccentricity,* but while the former suggests a personal peculiarity, often constitutional: *An allergy to vanilla was one of his idiosyncrasies;* the latter implies deviations from the usual or customary: *His eccentricity was to eat the dessert before the salad.*

imperceptible (im per SEP tuh b'l) Very slight, gradual, or subtle; not readily apparent: *The changes in his appearance had been almost imperceptible, but when she came across a photograph of how he had looked a year ago, she realized how different he was now;* not capable of being perceived: *Color is imperceptible to the blind.*

   imperceptibility (im per sep tuh BIL uh tee), the incapability of being perceived.

   imperceptibly (im per SEP tuh blee), in an imperceptible manner.

   A *perception* is a recognition of a physical object through the senses; or an intuitive recognition, as of a moral or aesthetic quality: *He found that he had arrived at a new perception of moral virtue through his study with the great theologian.*

impetuous (im PECH oo 's) Acting with or characterized by sudden rash energy: *When she finally came in sight, he made an impetuous dash across the street to meet her;* moving with great force; violent: *His impetuous words moved the crowds to surge forward, cheering.* The word comes from the noun impetus, a moving force or impulse.

   impetuosity (im pech oo AHS uh tee), impetuous quality or action: *His impetuosity was the despair of his nervous, conservative parents.* Also, **impetuousness.**

   impetuously (im PECH oo 's lee), in an impetuous manner.

   Impetuous and *impulsive* both refer to persons who are hasty, or to actions not preceded by thought. But while *impetuous* suggests eagerness, violence, or rashness, *impulsive* emphasizes spontaneity and lack of reflection.

implacable (im PLAY kuh b'l; im PLAAK uh b'l) Not to be appeased or pacified; incapable of being appeased: *Their implacable hostility toward each other never wavered the slightest through the years.*

   implacability (im play kuh BIL uh tee; im plaak uh BIL uh tee), refusal to be placated or appeased; disposition to be implacable: *His implacability in the face of her pleas was unyielding.* Also, **implacableness** (im PLAY kuh b'l n's; im PLAAK uh b'l n's).

   implacably (im PLAY kuh blee; im PLAAK uh blee), in an implacable manner.

implicit (im PLIS 't) Understood or suggested rather than expressed: *They had an implicit understanding about the future which did not require verbal promises;* virtually contained in, when followed by *in*: *His acceptance of their engagement was implicit in his announcement that he wanted to give a party for them.* When it refers to belief, confidence, or obedience, the word means unquestioning or unreserved: *She had implicit confidence in his integrity.*

The opposite of this is explicit, clearly expressed, leaving nothing in doubt, definite.

implicitly (im PLIS 't lee), without being expressed; in implicit manner: *They trusted each other implicitly in matters of judgment.*

implicitness (im PLIS 't n's), the condition of being implicit. This word is not used much, however.

improvident (im PRAHV uh d'nt) The *im-* shows that this is the negative form of the adjective provident, which comes from the same source as provide and means careful in providing for the future, or having or showing foresight. Improvident means neglecting to provide for the future, lacking in foresight, incautious: *the improvident way in which he squandered his inheritance, the country's improvident use of natural resources.*

improvidently (im PRAHV uh d'nt lee), in an improvident manner: *She improvidently gave away all sorts of things that she was tired of, never thinking she might have trouble replacing them later.*

improvidence (im PRAHV uh d'ns), the state or quality of being improvident: *His improvidence in financial matters finally brought him to dependence on his friends.*

inadvertent (in uhd VER t'nt) Needless; characterized by lack of attention; unintentional: *His inadvertent confusion of names caused him a good deal of embarrassment.* The -advert- in the word means turn to; thus inadvertent is failing to turn attention to.

inadvertence (in uhd VER t'ns), heedlessness, quality of being inadvertent: *By inadvertence, he neglected to sign his name,* an oversight: *This inadvertence almost cost him his job.* Also, **inadvertency**.

inadvertently (in uhd VER t'nt lee), heedlessly, unintentionally: *He inadvertently joggled her arm, causing her to spill the coffee.*

incongruous (in KAHN groo 's) Out of keeping or inappropriate: *Her suggestion that the fashion-show models parade to chamber music struck the committee members as incongruous;* inconsistent; not harmonious: *They made an incongruous couple, she so tall and gracious and he so short and fussy;* sometimes suggests absurdity.

incongruously (in KAHN groo 's lee), in an unsuitable or inconsistent manner: *The delicate watercolor and the bold painting were incongruously hanging next to each other.*

incongruity (in kun GROO uh tee), unsuitableness; inconsistency; lack of harmony: *She sensed the incongruity of putting fluffy ruffled curtains in that formal room;* something incongruous. Also, **incongruousness** (in KAHN groo 's n's).

increment (IN kruh m'nt) In addition or increase: *Over the years the increment to his resources was slow but steady;* act of increasing. The word is perhaps most often heard in relation to profit and money: *The promotion was reflected in a large increment to his annual earnings, by stock dividends as well as salary increase;* in other uses it is likely to sound too formal. The common phrase, *unearned increment,* refers to the increase in the value of property without effort on the part of the owner, such as increased demand because of population increase or movement, or a war-stimulated boom.

incremental (in kruh MEN t'l), pertaining to or resulting from increase or growth.

inexorable (in EK suh ruh b'l) Unyielding, unalterable: *It was an inexorable fact that he had been fired;* unmoved by persuasion or pleas: *He was inexorable in his refusal to consider the proposition.*

inexorably (in EK suh ruh blee), unyieldingly: *The armed guards moved inexorably toward the rabble.*

inexorability (in ek suh ruh BIL uh tee), unalterability, refusal to be moved: *the inexorability of the prime minister on the housing issue; inexorability of circumstances.*

Inexorable, implacable, and *inflexible* all have the quality of not being moved. But *inflexible* means unbending, following without deviation a set plan or purpose; *implacable* means incapable of being appeased; and *inexorable* means stern, unmoved by any plea.

inherent (in HEER 'nt; in HER 'nt) From the Latin word meaning to stick, which is the root of adherent, sticking *to;* sticking *in*—that is, existing *in* something as a permanent and inseparable part or quality: *The notion of impartiality is inherent in the conception of a judge. Stickiness is an inherent quality of flypaper.*

inherently (in HEER 'nt lee; in HER 'nt lee), by the nature of: *Sugar is inherently sweet.*

inhere (in HEER), the verb form, followed by *in;* to exist permanently and inseparably in: *Her beauty inheres in the lines of her face.*

inherence (in HEER 'ns; in HER 'ns), the state or fact of being inherent. Also, **inherency.**

innuendo (in yoo EN do) An indirect allusion or hint about a person or thing, especially if it suggests discredit: *It was hard to repair the damage to his reputation, since most of it had been caused not by direct charges, but by innuendo.* In law the term applies to a parenthetical explanation, particularly to the meaning of statements alleged to be harmful or libelous.

Insinuation, in its meaning of an artful suggestion not plainly stated, is almost synonymous, but *innuendo* has a stronger feeling of intention to cause injury by indirect allusion.

inordinate (in AWR d' n't) From the Latin for disordered, this means excessive, not within proper limits: *Her inordinate requirements for attention put a strain on the whole family;* disorderly; unrestrained in conduct: *His inordinate temper was always getting him into trouble.*

inordinately (in AWR d' n't lee), excessively, in an unrestrained manner: *She was so inordinately extravagant that he put her on a rigid allowance.*

inordinacy (in AWR d' nuh see), excessiveness; state or quality of being inordinate: *The inordinacy of his demands for the minor services he was to perform shocked them.* Also, **inordinateness** (in AWR duh n't n's).

insatiable (in SAY shuh b'l; in SAY shee uh b'l) Incapable of being satisfied: *His desire to hear music was so insatiable that he played records all day.*

insatiably (in SAY shuh blee; in SAY shee uh blee), in a manner suggesting incapability of being satisfied: *He devoured the fruit insatiably.*

insatiability (in say shuh BIL uh tee; in say shee uh BIL uh tee) incapability of being satisfied. Also, **insatiableness** (in SAY shuh b'l n's; in SAY shee uh b'l n's). These words are derivatives in the negative form of the verb *satiate,* to supply with anything to such a degree as to disgust or weary (from a Latin word meaning filled full). *Satiety* (suh TEYE uh tee), or *satiation,* is the state of being satiated. Both these words have a sense of excess which is not present in *satisfaction.* They imply merely fulfilling desires or needs to the degree that one is content. Although positive forms of these words exist—*satiable,* etc.—they are not commonly used.

insinuate (in SIN yoo ate) The meaning of the Latin source, *insinuatus,* brought in by windings and turnings, shows up in the meaning of this word, to bring artfully or subtly into someone's mind, to suggest or hint slyly: *He managed to insinuate into the mind of her employer the idea that she was unreliable;* or to introduce into a position or relation by indirect or artful methods: *Before they were aware of what was happening, they found that she had insinuated herself into a position of influence in the organization;* to make innuendoes: *He insinuated that the newcomer's background would not bear close investigation.*

insinuation (in sin yoo AY sh'n), veiled hint or artful suggestion, as of something not plainly stated: *an insinuation of bribery;* or ingratiation, the art or power of stealing into the affections: *She had so won him over by gentle insinuation that he missed her if she did not appear every day.*

insinuating (in SIN yoo ay ting), as an adjective, means winding or creeping quietly in; ingratiating: *the insinuating strains of the music.*

insinuatingly (in SIN yoo ay ting lee), in an insinuating manner.

insinuator (in SIN yoo ay t'r), one who insinuates.

instigate (IN stuh gate) The Latin word from which this comes means to prick. Instigate means to goad or spur to action. *He instigated his little sister to commit all sorts of mischief for which he denied responsibility;* to bring about by urging or spurring on: *He schemed to instigate disagreement so that he could step in and take control of the divided party.*

instigation (in stuh GAY sh'n), the act of spurring on or inciting: *The law suit was brought at his instigation.* Also, though not commonly, incentive.

instigator (IN stuh gay t'r), one who instigates: *The instigator of the rebellion was not even a member of the organization.*

instigative (IN stuh gay t'v), tending to instigate: *His fiery speeches were instigative to revolt.*

Instigate and its derivatives are usually associated with

urging to undesirable action, although this is not necessarily always the case. In this connotation it differs from *impel,* to drive or urge forward, with a sense of force or strong feeling; *induce,* to lead by persuasion or influence; or *incite,* to provoke or stir to action. This last is closest in meaning to *instigate,* but may be applied equally to good or bad actions: *He was incited by his dedication to the cause to heroic deeds he hadn't known he was capable of. Instigate* often suggests initiating or being at the source of action.

integrate (IN tuh grate) This word and all its derivatives are based on the mathematical term integer, meaning a whole number as distinguished from a fraction or a mixed number. Thus, to integrate means to bring together parts in a whole; or to make up or complete as a whole: *He hoped to integrate the parts of the chorus at the next rehearsal.*

  integration (in tuh GRAY sh'n), the noun meaning combination into a whole. *The integration of the several disagreeing factions into a smoothly operating organization would probably take many months.* In psychology it means the organization of personality traits into an orderly and effective functioning; behavior in harmony with the environment: *Her adaptability and friendliness quickly helped her to achieve a satisfying integration into the new community.*

  integrator (IN tuh gray t'r), one who or that which integrates.
  integrative (IN tuh gray t'v), tending to integrate.
  integral (IN tuh gr'l), of or pertaining to or composing a whole: *the integral elements of a university;* necessary to the completeness of the whole: *The use of that form in that place is integral to the composition of the picture.*

  integrity (in TEG ruh tee). From the idea of wholeness contained in this word comes the sense of soundness of principle and character, honesty—that is, moral wholeness: *Even though suspicion fell on his associates, his own integrity remained unquestioned.* It may also mean the state of being whole, undiminished, or perfect: *The integrity of the nation was never so gravely threatened as in the Civil War.*

  Integration and *integrate* have taken on special meanings in the United States since the Supreme Court decision of 1954, requiring that public facilities be unified into a single system, with no separation or exclusion on the basis of race or color. *Integration* is the term used for the combining of previously segregated or separate facilities—for education, transportation, etc.—provided for blacks with those of whites. An *integrationist* is one who supports this philosophy; a *segregationist,* one who opposes it.

Disintegrate, the opposite of integrate, is to reduce to fragments, to destroy the cohesion of, to break down into separate elements: *He spent a great deal of time trying to disintegrate the compound so that he could analyze it. Under the pressure of poverty and illness, the family would have disintegrated without help.*

intrepid (in TREP 'd) The Latin root of this word means alarmed or agitated; combined with *in-,* meaning not, it gives the sense of fearless, dauntless: *an intrepid explorer, an intrepid soul.*

   intrepidity (in truh PID uh tee), fearless bravery.

   intrepidly (in TREP 'd lee), fearlessly.

   trepidation (trep uh DAY sh'n). The Latin verb from which this comes means to hurry with alarm or to tremble, and the first meaning of this word was a vibratory movement, or trembling. Its more common meaning, however, is a quaking fear or state of alarm: *Her trepidation under her uncle's cold, accusing stare was pitiful to behold.*

   Trepid and *trepidity,* the positive forms of *intrepid* and *intrepidity,* are not in common use.

inveterate (in VET uh r't) Its common source with veteran, one who is experienced through long service or practice, is apparent. It means confirmed in a feeling, habit, or practice through long continuance: *an inveterate liar;* strongly established: *In spite of all his failures, he had an inveterate optimism. Her inveterate addiction to detective stories rather amused her friends.* It may also mean obstinate or inflexible: *His inveterate insistence on maintaining the family traditions placed a great burden on his grandchildren;* suggesting an unreasonable attachment to undesirable or unpleasant habits or qualities: *He is an inveterate thief.*

   inveterately (in VET uh r't lee), in a persistent manner: *He was inveterately attached to the old summer place.*

   inveterateness (in VET uh r't n's), persistence.

   inveteracy (in VET uh ruh see), deep-rootedness, obstinacy. *The inveteracy of his gambling was the despair of his family.*

irrevocable (ih REV uh kuh b'l) Not to be recalled, repealed, or annulled: *Despite their pleas, he insisted his decision was irrevocable;* a derivative of revoke, to call or take back, to withdraw.

   irrevocably (ih REV uh kuh blee), in such a way as to be beyond recall or reversal: *She was irrevocably committed to her project.*

irrevocability (ih rev uh kuh BIL uh tee), the quality or condition of being irrevocable: *The irrevocability of this right was provided for in the charter.* Also, **irrevocableness**.

Without the prefix *in-* (which becomes *ir-* before *-r*) these words all have the opposite or positive meaning, as *revocable*, capable of being recalled or reversed. A number of words are built upon the root of *-vok-*, from the Latin *vocaré*, to call. *Evoke* is to call forth or produce: *The snapshot evoked old memories;* or to call up in the sense of causing to appear: *to evoke a spirit.* The noun, *evocation*, is the act of evoking; the adjective *evocative*, tending to evoke. *Invoke* is to call for with earnest desire: *to invoke his master's pity;* to appeal to, as for confirmation: *to invoke the rules;* or to call forth or call upon by magic or ritual: *Aladdin invoked the genie by rubbing his lamp.* The act of invoking, the entreaty or formula, is *invocation*. To *provoke* is to call forth in the sense of stir up, arouse, stimulate to action, or exasperate: *to provoke anger, provoke a response, provoke his father.* The adjective meaning tending to provoke, inciting or stimulating, is *provocative: a provocative idea, a woman's provocative manner.* The adverb is *provocatively* and the noun, *provocativeness*.

itinerant (eye TIN uh r'nt; ih TIN uh r'nt) From the Latin word for journey, this means traveling from place to place, or on a circuit: *an itinerant preacher; itinerant circus;* or one who travels from place to place, especially for duty or business: *Being itinerants, the fruit-pickers never stay long enough in one place to make a home.*

itinerancy (eye TIN uh r'n see; ih TIN uh r'n see), the act or state of traveling from place to place: *Itinerancy is a condition of a traveling missionary's work.*

itinerary (eye TIN uh rair ee; ih TIN uh rair ee), the route followed on a journey: *They planned the itinerary to allow plenty of time for sightseeing;* an account or record of travel: *He kept his itinerary in good order by making daily entries;* or a book describing a route of travel, with information for travelers: *Baedeker's itineraries were the traveler's authority in the nineteenth century.*

itinerate (eye TIN uh rate; ih TIN uh rate), to go from place to place, especially in a regular circuit, as in preaching; not in frequent use.

jeopardize (JEP 'r dize) To put in danger or expose to risk: *He jeopardized his own life in rescuing the child from the water. Any failure of coördination would jeopardize the success of the plan.*

jeopardy (JEP 'r dee), danger, risk: *He knew he was putting his whole future in jeopardy by extending his credit to the limit to buy into the venture*. In law it has the special meaning of the danger of being found guilty and suffering the consequences to which an accused person is exposed: *A person freed from a murder charge cannot be put in double jeopardy by being tried again for the same murder*.

jettison (JET ih s'n) This word was once specifically associated with water, and meant to throw cargo or movable objects overboard to lighten a vessel in distress—that is, to make flotsam and jetsam of it. It has come to mean getting rid of any obstacle or burden: *He decided to jettison the whole plan and start over again. She tried to jettison her painful memories by throwing away all her old letters*.

jetsam (JET s'm), actually another form of jettison, is the material that is cast overboard to lighten a ship. It is almost always associated with *flotsam* though technically distinguished from it. Jetsam is what was purposely thrown out to lighten the vessel; *flotsam*, the part of the wreckage of a ship and its cargo found floating on the sea. The phrase *flotsam and jetsam* may signify simply odds and ends, wreckage, junk, carrying with it the sense of something aimless or ignored.

jocular (JAHK yuh l'r) The Latin word for little joke is the source for this word, meaning given to joking, playful, humorous: *His jocular remarks seemed out of place in those solemn surroundings;* characterized by, intended for, or suited to jesting: *The jocular tone of his little speech was refreshing to an audience which had already heard several serious lectures*.

jocularity (jahk yuh LAAR uh tee), state or quality of being jocular: *The jocularity of his answer belittled the seriousness of the question*.

jocularly (JAHK yuh l'r lee), in a joking manner.

A number of other words having similar meanings begin with the same syllable. *Jocose* (jo KOSE, JO kose) is just about the same as *jocular;* both suggest heavy-handedness, and both are rather bookish terms. The noun is *jocosity,* or *jocoseness;* the adverb, *jocosely*. *Jovial* has more the sense of hearty good humor and goodfellowship: *His jovial presence sparked the whole party*. *Joviality* or *jovialness* are the nouns; *jovially,* the adverb. *Jocund* (JAHK 'nd, JO k'nd) is cheerful or merry, suggesting lightheartedness; the noun is *jocundity*. This is now a literary word, not usually heard in ordinary speech.

juxtapose (juks tuh POZE; JUKS tuh poze) Formed from the word element *juxta-*, near to or beside, and *-pose*, to place, this means to place side by side or very close to: *By juxtaposing the two tables, he was able to see that one was a little higher than the other.*

juxtaposition (juks tuh puh ZISH 'n), a placing close together: *The printer's juxtaposition of various styles of type in one sample was useful in helping them choose one;* position side by side: *The dramatic juxtaposition of extreme poverty and great luxury characterizes cities which have enjoyed sudden prosperity.*

kleptomania (klep tuh MAY nee yuh) An irresistible desire to steal without regard to personal needs; a persistent impulse of neurotic origin in which the object stolen usually has some special significance; from the Greek for steal, plus *mania*, a madness or uncontrollable zeal: *Her kleptomania took the form of stealing handkerchiefs.*

kleptomaniac (klep tuh MAY nee aak), as a noun, one affected with kleptomania; as an adjective, relating to or characteristic of kleptomania.

lacerate (LAAS uh rate) In the physical sense, this means to tear roughly, to mangle: *He was badly lacerated trying to escape under the barbed wire.* From this also developed the meaning to hurt or cause sharp pain, not necessarily physically: *The bitter argument lacerated her emotions.*

laceration (laas uh RAY sh'n), the act of lacerating: *The evidences of laceration on the body pointed to the killer who had been wandering about the area in the last month;* or the result of lacerating: *He suffered lacerations from broken glass in the accident.*

languid (LAANG gwid) Faint from weakness or fatigue: *My illness had left me almost too languid to move;* lacking in spirit or energy, dull, slack: *She was too languid to be good company on the kind of outdoor excursions he enjoyed.*

languidly (LAANG gwid lee), in a sluggish manner.

languidness (LAANG gwid n's), the quality or state of being languid.

languish (LAANG gwish), to become weak, lose vigor: *They began to languish in the tropical climate;* to suffer under unfavorable conditions: *He was left to languish in prison;* to assume an expression of tender, sentimental melancholy: *Much to his* *embarrassment, she languished at him so obviously that the others could not fail to notice;* to pine for: *It used to be fashionable for maidens to languish after their absent lovers.* Except in the first two meanings, this is becoming a humorous literary word, a rather affected one.

languishment (LAANG gwish m'nt), the act of languishing, or a languishing condition.

languor (LAANG g'r), physical weakness or lack of energy; emotional softness or tenderness: *As she thought of him she was filled with delicious languor;* a soothing or oppressive stillness: *The languor of early evening seemed to make the house unusually quiet.*

Languishing and *languorous* have in common with *languid* the sense of weakness and lack of spirit or energy. In *languid* the sense is of inability to exert oneself because of weakness due to illness or fatigue; in *languishing,* there is more of a sense of indolence or boredom paralyzing action; in *languorous,* the implication is of self-indulgence and emotionalism.

Lethargic (luh THAHR jik) is another adjective suggesting sluggish inactivity, but in this case caused by drowsiness. *Listless* implies lack of interest combined with appearance of languor.

loquacious (lo KWAY sh's) Inclined to talk much or freely, from the Latin verb meaning to talk: *Although an interesting conversationalist, he was so loquacious that you encouraged him at your risk;* wordy.

loquaciously (lo KWAY sh's lee), in a loquacious manner.

loquaciousness (lo KWAY sh's n's), talkativeness, quality of being loquacious: *Her loquaciousness first overwhelmed her listeners, then bored them.* Also, **loquacity** (lo KWAAS uh tee).

lucid (LOO sid) The several meanings of this word all derive from the Latin root meaning light. It means bright or shining; clear; transparent, in a physical sense: *The lucid brook reflected the overhanging trees;* easily understood: *His lucid demonstration suddenly brought all the elements of the problem into proper relation;* characterized by clear perception or understanding, rational: *In his lucid phases, he was a delightful companion.*

lucidly (LOO sid lee), clearly, in a manner clearly understood: *She expressed her ideas more lucidly in writing than in speaking.*

lucidity (loo SID ih tee), the quality of being lucid, especially in thought or style: *The lucidity of her argument won over many who had been previously undecided.*

The verb *elucidate* means to make clear or throw light on: *He elucidated his position to the satisfaction of his listeners. Elucidation* is the act or means of elucidating. It is also an explanation.

luxuriant (lug ZHOOR ee 'nt; luk SHOOR ee 'nt) Growing abundantly or richly: *The luxuriant growth of flowers in the tropics always surprises visitors from other parts of the world;* elaborate, as applied to style or expression, with the suggestion of excess: *The luxuriant detail of the carving was a marvel of delicacy.*

 luxuriantly (lug ZHOOR ee 'nt lee; luk SHOOR ee 'nt lee), in a luxuriant manner.

 luxuriance (lug ZHOOR ee 'ns; luk SHOOR ee 'ns), the condition of being luxuriant; rich growth: *the luxuriance of his beard;* productiveness.

 Luxuriant should be distinguished from *luxurious,* with which it is often confused. *Luxurious* is unrestrained indulgence in enjoyment or the refined pleasures of living: *Her luxurious villa was always open to her friends; he kept showering her with luxurious gifts.* The verb *luxuriate* means to indulge in luxury, or to take great delight in something: *to luxuriate in a warm bath.* Its first meaning, however, was to grow abundantly, to flourish, which provides the connecting link between *luxuriant* and *luxurious.*

malignant (muh LIG n'nt) This word and all its derivatives and related words are from the Latin word meaning evil, the combining form *male-* being the opposite of *bene-,* good. Malignant means desirous of or taking pleasure in causing suffering or injury: *Her well-known malignant disposition frightened everyone;* dangerous or harmful: *He was determined to trace to their source the malignant rumors of his financial instability.* In the medical sense, it means tending to produce death: *a malignant growth.*

 malignance (muh LIG n'ns), quality or state of being malignant; vicious ill-will. Also, malignancy. This latter form is also the term for a malignant growth.

 malignantly (muh LIG n'nt lee), in a malignant manner, with intent to do harm.

 malign (muh LINE) as an adjective is essentially the same as malignant; showing an evil disposition, or evil in effect, although the sense emphasizes the unfavorable effect slightly more than the vicious intent: *A malign influence seemed to govern his business ventures.* As a verb it means to speak ill of or slander: *He claimed he had been maligned by the newspaper, and announced his intention to sue.*

malevolent (muh LEV uh l'nt) is an adjective implying, like malignant, wishing harm to others: *His malevolent expression warned his visitor that the interview would be unpleasant;* however, it suggests a smoldering state, not as likely to incite to action as *malignant,* which has the sense of deep intensity. The noun is *malevolence.*

malicious (muh LISH 's), another similar adjective meaning desirous of inflicting injury or suffering on another, emphasizes the intent; in fact, in law it specifically means motivated by vicious, wanton, or mischievous purposes: *She took malicious delight in spreading the gossip.* The nouns are *malice* (MAL is) and *maliciousness.*

maleficent (muh LEF uh s'nt), doing evil or harm, emphasizes the doing rather than the feeling or intention: *They knew the enemy had maleficent designs on them.* Malefic (muh LEF ik) is productive of evil, but it is a rather literary word. *Maleficence* (muh LEF uh s'ns) is the doing of evil or harm, or harmful character: *His maleficence over the years made everyone, not just his victims, dislike him.*

mediate (MEE dee ate) The Latin root of this word, to be in the middle, gives the essential meaning; to act between parties; to effect agreement or reconciliation: *The president appointed him to mediate because of his special knowledge of the background of the dispute. He always mediated differences between the board and the faculty;* or to act as a go-between; to convey something: *To mediate the good feeling between the two countries was his deepest wish.*

mediator (MEE dee ay t'r), one who mediates between parties in disagreement.

mediation (mee dee AY sh'n), action in mediating between parties: *His quiet mediation in the delicate affair won him an ambassadorship.*

mediative (MEE dee uh tiv), serving to mediate: *mediative intentions.*

meretricious (mair uh TRISH 's) This word is from a Latin one which means pertaining to or characteristic of a prostitute, and this was also its original meaning in English. It has come to mean tempting with false attractions, or cheaply showy; pretending to be something else; concealing something evil: *Such mere-tricious arguments should be exposed before they take in any more victims. Her charms were meretricious.*

meretriciously (mair uh TRISH 's lee), in a meretricious manner.

meretriciousness (mair uh TRISH 's n's), the state or quality of being meretricious: *the meretriciousness of his position.*

These words are often misused to mean just the opposite because of the apparent association with *merit* in the sound. It is important to remember that the spelling of the first two syllables is different.

misanthropy (mis AAN thruh pee) From *mis-*, a prefix meaning ill, mistaken, or wrong, and *anthropo-* a word element meaning man; signifies hatred or distrust of mankind: *One must assume that his misanthropy has its roots in his unhappy childhood and his unfortunate marriage.*

misanthrope (MIS 'n throp; MIZ 'n throp), a hater of mankind: *He's such a misanthrope that he's never very agreeable company.* Also, **misanthropist** (mis AAN thruh pist).

misanthropic (mis 'n THROP ik), characterized by hatred or contempt for mankind; avoiding association with others: *His misanthropic observations were bitterly witty.*

Philanthropy (fi LAAN thruh pee), by contrast, is love of mankind, derived from *phil-* meaning love. The word has come to have a more specific meaning of goodwill as expressed in good deeds and charity, the promotion of human welfare. A *philanthropist* is one who performs such good deeds. His or her actions and intentions are called *philanthropic.*

modulate (MAHJ uh late) The source is a Latin word meaning to measure; to regulate or adjust to a certain measure or proportion: *Her well-modulated voice carried perfectly in the hall;* to soften or tone down: *He realized he would have to modulate the tone of his address for this obviously conservative audience.*

modulation (mahj uh LAY sh'n), regulation or adjustment to a certain measure or proportion: *The modulation of his attitude to one closer to theirs was gratifying to his colleagues;* variation or inflection of the voice: *The modulations of her voice gave new meaning to the poetry.*

modulator (MAHJ uh lay t'r), one who or that which modulates.

momentous (mo MEN t's) This adjective comes from the meaning of moment in the sense of importance or seriousness; hence it means of grave importance; having possible serious or far-reaching consequences: *Landing on the moon was one of the most momentous events in the history of this country.*

momentousness (mo MEN t's n's), seriousness, importance: *The momentousness of the president's words alarmed everyone.*

momentously (mo MEN t's lee), in a serious manner, a manner suggesting grave consequences.

Momentary (MO m'n tair ee), which is sometimes confused with *momentous,* is the adjective derived from the sense of *moment* as an instant. It means very brief: *a momentary twinge of pain;* or occurring at any moment: *She expected his momentary arrival. Momentarily* (mo m'n TAIR uh lee) is the adverb: *She expected him momentarily.*

morbid (MAWR bid) From the Latin word meaning sickly, unwholesome, this has essentially the same meaning in English. It may mean affected by or characteristic of disease: *morbid fatigue;* or more commonly, unwholesomely gloomy or sensitive, suggesting an unhealthy mental state: *She had a morbid interest in funerals which led her to read the obituary columns first.*

morbidity (mawr BID uh tee), state or quality of being morbid: *The morbidity of his remarks startled his friends, who usually found him cheerful.* It may also refer to the proportion of sickness in a locality: *The morbidity rate for measles was much higher than in the neighboring towns.* Also, **morbidness,** in the first sense.

morbidly (MAWR b'd lee), in a morbid manner.

Mordant (MAWR d'nt) is an adjective with the same gloomy cast as *morbid,* but it means biting or sarcastic with the suggestion of bitterness: *Those who offended became the butts of his mordant wit. Mordancy* (MAWR d'n see) is a sharp, sarcastic quality of feeling, style, or expression.

munificent (myoo NIF uh s'nt) Extremely generous, lavish in giving: *He enjoyed playing the role of the munificent benefactor to his friends;* characterized by great generosity: *He left a number of munificent bequests to various charities.*

munificence (myoo NIF uh s'ns), lavish generosity: *The elegant furnishings of the club testified to his munificence.*

munificently (myoo NIF uh s'nt lee), in a munificent manner.

nauseous (NAW sh's; NAW zee's) This adjective is from nausea, taken directly from the Greek word for seasickness. Nauseous means causing nausea, stomach-turning; sickening in the sense of being disgusting: *She had a nauseous moment when she saw the wormy food. The nauseous smells of the sick-room.* Also, **nauseating.**

    nauseously (NAW sh's lee: NAW zee's lee), in a nauseous manner: *She was affected nauseouly by the vulgar display.*

    nauseousness (NAW sh's n's; NAW zee's n's), the state or quality of being nauseous: *the nauseousness of the hot, crowded room.*

    The verb related to these words is *nauseate* (NAW shee ate; NAW zee ate), to affect with nausea, sicken, feel extreme disgust. When one says he is *nauseated,* therefore, he means he is affected with nausea, sickened. It is now common to hear *nauseated* in this sense used interchangeably with *nauseous,* although the latter usually means sickening, not sickened.

nebulous (NEB yuh l's) In astronomy, a nebula is a cloudy luminous mass: from this we have the meaning of the adjective cloudy or cloud-like, hence hazy, indistinct, vague, or confused: *She had only a nebulous recollection of what had happened. The longer they argued the more nebulous the distinctions seemed to become.*

    nebulosity (neb yuh LAHS uh tee), a nebulous state: *The nebulosity of his status made him very uncomfortable;* or nebulous matter. Also, **nebulousness.**

    nebulously (NEB yuh l's lee), in vague, indistinct manner.

negotiable (nuh GO shuh b'l) Derived from the Latin word for business, the strictest meaning of this word is transferable by delivery (referring to bills, notes, etc.) with or without endorsement, with the title going to the receiving party: *He insisted that she endorse all the checks at once so that they would be negotiable.* From this it has come to mean capable of being transacted or dealt with. Thus, one can speak of a road being negotiable only under certain conditions: *It is not negotiable in the rain;* or of certain conditions to an agreement not being negotiable—that is, not open to bargaining, not able to be used as payment for some concession by the other side.

    negotiability (nuh go shuh BIL uh tee), the quality or state of being negotiable: *The negotiability of the bonds made her uneasy about keeping them at home.*

    negotiate (nuh GO shee ate), to deal with others, as in preparing a treaty or business transaction: *He anticipated some difficult problems in negotiating for the oil leases;* to arrange by discussion and consideration of terms: *They felt he had negoti-*

ated a very favorable settlement; to get around an obstacle: *She negotiated the hill with some difficulty;* to conclude certain kinds of financial transactions: *negotiate securities.*

negotiation (nuh go shee AY sh'n), mutual discussion and arrangement of the terms of a transaction or agreement: *The strike negotiations went on through the night;* the action or process of negotiating.

negotiator (nuh GO shee ay t'r), one who negotiates.

noisome (NOY s'm) Related not to noise but to annoy, this means offensive or disgusting, especially in reference to odor: *The old man was found in a room so neglected and noisome, he could not be properly cared for there.* It may also mean harmful or injurious: *The noisome environment was hampering her recovery.*

noisomeness (NOY s'm n's), offensiveness, harmfulness.

noisomely (NOY s'm lee), in a noisome manner: *The heavy, reeking atmosphere of the market place began to press in on her noisomely.*

nutrition (nyoo TRISH 'n; noo TRISH 'n) From the same Latin word as nourish, this is the act or process of nourishing or being nourished, or the process by which food material taken into a living organism is used: *The nutrition of infants is of the greatest importance for their future development.*

nutritious (nyoo TRISH 's; noo TRISH 's), nourishing, promoting growth: *Too many trees on a lawn rob the soil of nutritious elements necessary for grass.*

nutritiousness (nyoo TRISH 's n's; noo TRISH 's n's), the quality or state of being nutritous: *The nutritiousness of the diet was demonstrated in the experiment.*

nutritiously (nyoo TRISH 's lee; noo TRISH 's lee) in a nutritious manner.

nutritionist (nyoo TRISH 'n ist; noo TRISH 'n ist), one who studies problems of food and nutrition.

nutritive (NYOO truh t'v'; NOO truh t'v), the same as nutritious in one sense, but it also means of or concerned in nutrition: *nutritive elements in various foods.*

nutriment (NYOO truh m'nt; NOO truh m'nt), nourishment, food, whatever serves to sustain an organism in its existence: *Cast away on the island, they had to take their nutriment from many strange plants and fruits.*

nutrient (NYOO tree 'nt, NOO tree 'nt), affording nutriment: *He was working on a synthetic compound of nutrient elements suitable for corn.*

Nourishment and *nutrition* are essentially synonymous, although *nutrition* may also refer to the actual physical process of using the *nutriment* absorbed by an organism. However, there is no verb to correspond to *nourish,* to sustain with food or nutriment. It also has a broader meaning, to foster or promote: *She was privately nourishing a plan to study abroad.*

obeisance (O BAY s'ns; O BEE s'ns) There is an apparent relationship to obey, and this word did once mean obedience. Now, however, it refers to the physical act of expressing respect by bowing, bending, or prostrating oneself before a superior or one entitled to such a sign: *Those awaiting the Pope made obeisance as he entered;* and more generally it is an attitude of respect: *He made a mental obeisance to this great mind whose inspiring words he had been reading.*

> **obeisant** (O BAY s'nt; O BEE s'nt), bowing in respect, treating with deference: *He was obeisant to her demands, unreasonable as they were.*
> **obeisantly** (O BAY s'nt lee; O BEE s'nt lee), in an obeisant manner.

obfuscate (ahb FUS kate; AHB f's kate) The sense of to darken, from the Latin, carries over into the meaning of making obscure, to confuse, to make unnecessarily difficult: *He had a way of obfuscating the real issue by introducing all sorts of unimportant considerations.*

> **obfuscation** (ahb f's KAY sh'n), the quality or state of being obfuscated: *It was easy to see how the obfuscation of the original purpose had come about;* or an act or instance of obfuscating something: *This deliberate obfuscation of what the financial statement means cannot be tolerated.*
> **obfuscatory** (ahb FUS kuh tawr ee), tending to obfuscate: *obfuscatory tactics.*

obligatory (uh BLIG uh tawr ee) The elements of the Latin word from which this comes mean to tie over or against, hence this means binding, in the sense of being morally or legally required: *I feel it is obligatory for me to go to the meeting, since they are depending on me;* it may even mean compulsory: *In many colleges it is obligatory to go to chapel.*

> **obligatorily** (uh blig uh TAWR uh lee), in an obligatory manner.
> **obligation** (ahb luh GAY sh'n), a morally or legally binding requirement, duty, or promise: *She felt the obligation to com-*

plete her work before she left for her new job. Tax obligations; the state or fact of being indebted for a benefit or service: *Their kindness to him during his illness put him under heavy obligation.*

obligate (AHB luh gate), to bind morally or legally: *The builder was obligated under the zoning ordinance to provide certain safety features.*

oblige (uh BLIJE) is a broader verb than obligate, implying a requirement either to do or not to do something by law, command, duty, or necessity: *The strike at the auto plant obliged many dealers to disappoint their customers.* It may also mean to put under a debt of gratitude for a service or benefit: *I am much obliged for your thoughtfulness;* or to favor or accommodate: *They obliged the host by performing for the other guests.*

obliging (uh BLEYE jing), disposed to do favors or services: *It is good business practice for new enterprises to be especially obliging to potential customers.*

obligingly (uh BLEYE jing lee), in an obliging manner.

oblivious (uh BLIV ee 's) This may mean forgetful; without remembrance: *He was so good-natured, he must have been oblivious of past refusals;* heedless, unmindful or unconscious of: *oblivious to the noise; oblivious of the demands.*

obliviousness (uh BLIV ee 's n's), quality or state of being oblivious: *Her obliviousness to the traffic almost caused an accident.*

obliviously (uh BLIV ee 's lee), in an oblivious manner.

oblivion (uh BLIV ee un), the state of being forgotten: *The announcement of his death emphasized the years of oblivion after the accident which caused his retirement from public life;* or the forgetting or forgetfulness of something: *She looked forward to the sedative which would bring her temporary oblivion.*

obnoxious (ub NAHK sh's; ahb NAHK sh's) The *-noxious* part of this word means harmful, and the whole word therefore means harmful towards, in the direction of; objectionable; offensive: *His obnoxious behavior at the party caused some of the guests to leave early.*

obnoxiously (ub NAHK sh's lee; ahb NAHK sh's lee), in an obnoxious manner.

obnoxiousness (ub NAHK sh's n's; ahb NAHK sh's n's), state or quality of being obnoxious: *She determined to spare herself the obnoxiousness of his attentions by going away.*

Noxious by itself, means harmful, but more in a physical than in a moral sense: *noxious fumes; noxious waste material.*

obsession (ub SESH 'n; ahb SESH 'n) A dominating action or influence of a persistent idea or feeling, usually unreasonable, but inescapable. The Latin word from which it comes means besieged or beset; a person with an obsession cannot free himself of it: *Her obsession about never traveling alone often complicated her arrangements.* It may also mean the state of being obsessed, or the act of obsessing: *In his obsession with detail, he often overlooked larger matters.*

   obsess (ub SES; ahb SES), to beset, trouble, or dominate: *She knew the problem would obsess her until she solved it.*

   obsessive (ub SES 'v; ahb SES 'v), relating to or characterized by obsession; being excessive in some quality almost to the point of abnormality: *an obsessive preoccupation with her appearance.* Also, **obsessional** (ub SESH uh n'l; ahb SESH uh n'l).

   obsessively (ub SES 'v lee; ahb SES 'v lee), in an obsessive manner.

   Obsession is sometimes confused with similar psychological terms which suggest that there is no rational basis for the states they describe. A *compulsion* is a strong impulse to carry out an irrational act, a *phobia*, a morbid fear or dread.

officious (uh fISH 's) Originally this meant willing to serve, and implied helpful, kindly attention. Now it has come to mean forward in volunteering services where they are not wanted or needed and has an unpleasant connotation: *Everyone warned her about the officious advice she was sure to get from the past president.*

   officiously (uh fISH 's lee), in an officious manner.

   officiousness (uh fISH 's n's), officious quality or behavior: *The board disliked his officiousness in speaking for them without their authority.* This word must be distinguished from the adjective *official*, which means pertaining to an office, duty, or position; or authorized. Thus, the essential difference is that *official* means with authority, *officious* without.

orthodox (AWR thuh dahks) From the Greek *ortho-*, meaning straight, right, and *-dox*, opinion, belief, this signifies soundness in opinion or belief, especially religious doctrine. Implied in this is adherence to some established authority, standard, or tradition: *Her methods of teaching were orthodox, if not inspired.* More specifically, it means conforming to a faith as represented in the church creeds. It also has the broader meaning of approved, conventional, conservative: *His orthodox designs had been very successful in the past, but now his young associates* *were eager to try a new approach.* When capitalized, the word refers to a particular religious organization or group, as the Greek Orthodox Church.

orthodoxy (AWR thuh dahk see), orthodox belief or practice: *Her orthodoxy in matters of etiquette seemed amusing to her grandchildren;* orthodox character: *orthodoxy of economic views.*

orthodoxly (AWR thuh dahks lee), in an orthodox manner.

ostensible (ahs TEN suh b'l) Apparent or outwardly appearing, usually with the implication that the appearance does not represent the true state of affairs; thus, pretended: *His ostensible purpose in taking charge of her affairs was to protect her, but actually he was using her money for risky dealings of his own.*

ostensibly (ahs TEN suh blee), in an ostensible manner, to all outward appearances: *Ostensibly an objective statement of the main campaign issues, this pamphlet cleverly discredits the other candidate.*

Ostensible (from the Latin word meaning to show) may sometimes be confused with *ostentatious* (from a related Latin word meaning to display). *Ostentatious* means showy, particularly in a way intended to impress others: *He always made ostentatious references to the important people he was on familiar terms with.*

ostracize (AHS truh size) In ancient Greece, a citizen could be temporarily banished by public vote with ballots consisting of broken pieces of earthen vessels, called *ostraka*. From this comes ostracize, to exclude from society, or from certain privileges, by general consent: *There was an unspoken agreement to ostracize him from the group for his crude behavior.*

ostracism (AHS truh sizm), the act of ostracizing, or the fact or state of being ostracized: *He knew that his outspoken views might condemn him to professional ostracism by his colleagues.*

paragon (PAAR uh gahn) A model or pattern of excellence, or a particular excellence: *At school he had been such a paragon of learning and proper behavior that he was heartily disliked by the other boys.*

pendulous (PEN juh l's; PEN dyuh l's) Related to pendulum, a body suspended from a fixed point so as to move back and forth by the action of gravity and acquired momentum. A pendulum is most commonly represented by the swinging device used to control the movement of clockwork. This adjective, then, means hanging or swinging freely: *She was wearing an armful of bracelets with pendulous ornaments.*

pendulously (PEN juh l's lee; PEN dyuh l's lee), in pendulous fashion. It would be rather strained, however, to use this adverb.

pendulousness (PEN juh l's n's; PEN dyuh l's n's), the state or quality of hanging loose.

pendulum (PEN juh l'm; PEN dyuh l'm)

The root *-pend-*, from the Latin meaning to weigh, appears in many related words as in *depend, impend,* and *suspend. Pending* means hanging in the sense of being *suspended,* therefore undecided, awaiting conclusion or decision. A *pendant* is a hanging object, often ornamental. The adjective is spelled *pendent,* and means hanging or suspended. *Append* is to add on as an accessory, and has as derivatives *appendix,* additional explanatory matter, and *appendage,* a subordinate, attached part of anything.

permeate (PER mee ate) To pass through the substance or mass of something, to penetrate every part through pores or other openings. It may apply to something physical: *The dye did not permeate the fabric evenly;* or nonphysical: *His religious convictions permeated all his thinking.*

permeable (PER mee uh b'l), capable of being permeated: *The material was not permeable to oil.* The opposite is **impermeable.**

permeability (per mee uh BIL uh tee), the property or state of being permeable: *Tests were being carried out with the new synthetic to determine its permeability to liquid.* The opposite is **impermeability.**

permeance (PER mee 'ns), the act of permeating.

permeation (per mee AY sh'n), the quality or state of being permeated: *The permeation of these ideas through the nation took a surprisingly short time.*

perspicacity (per spuh KAAS uh tee) Originally meaning keenness of sight, this word has moved from the physical to the figurative. It now means keenness of mental perception, penetration, quick-wittedness: *His perspicacity in analyzing new situations quickly caught the attention of his superiors.* Also, **perspicaciousness** (per spuh KAY sh's n's).

perspicacious (per spuh KAY sh's), mentally keen, quick of perception: *She was so perspicacious in her studies she was able to graduate a year ahead of the usual time.*

perspicaciously (per spuh KAY sh's lee), in a perspicacious manner.

This word is to be distinguished from *perspicuous* (per SPIK yoo 's), clear to the understanding, or clear in expression or statement: *He made an outstandingly perspicuous statement of the issues confronting them.*

phlegmatic (fleg MAAT ik) The word derives its meanings from the old belief that phlegm was one of the four fluids, or humors, of the body. Being cold and moist, it was thought to cause apathy or sluggishness of disposition when it was predominant. It means not easily excited or moved to action or feeling; sluggish; self-possessed: *He was so phlegmatic that she couldn't tell if he was happy or sad.*

phlegmatically (fleg MAAT ik 'lee), in a phlegmatic manner.

placate (PLAY kate; PLAAK ate) To appease or soothe: *He was not easily placated when things went against him.*

placation (play KAY sh'n; pluh KAY sh'n), an act of soothing or pacifying: *She prepared all the foods he liked in her attempts at placation.*

placatory (PLAY kuh tor ee; PLAAK uh tor ee), tending, or intended to placate: *placatory strategy to win them over.* Also, **placating.**

placatingly (PLAY kay ting lee; PLAAK ay ting lee), in a placating manner.

placable (PLAY kuh b'l; PLAAK uh b'l), capable of being placated. The opposite is **implacable.**

placability (play kuh BIL uh tee; plaak uh BIL uh tee), the quality or state of being placable. Also, **placableness.** The opposites are **implacability** and **implacableness,** which are used much more often than their positive forms.

plagiarize (PLAY jee uh rize; PLAY juh rize) To copy or imitate the language, ideas, and thoughts of another author and pass them off as original work: *He admitted that he had plagiarized the material, believing the source was so obscure no one would discover it.*

plagiarism (PLAY jee uh rizm; PLAY juh rizm), an act or instance of plagiarizing; something taken from a plagiarized work: *Only a fool would have attempted to pass off this obvious plagiarism as original.* Also, **plagiary.**

plagiarist (PLAY jee uh rist; PLAY juh rist), one who plagiarizes. Also, **plagiarizer.**

plagiaristic (play jee uh RIS tik; play juh RIS tik), characterizing plagiarism: *plagiaristic use of his arguments and conclusion.*

platitude (PLAAT ih tyood; PLAAT ih tood) The *plat-* in this word means flat. A platitude is a flat, dull, trite remark, often uttered as if it were fresh and profound: *His speeches are so full of platitudes no one pays any attention to them any more.*

platitudinous (plaat ih TYOO d 'n 's; plaat ih TOO d 'n 's), characterized by or given to platitudes: *a platitudinous old bore;* of the nature of a platitude: *a platitudinous observation.*

platitudinously (plaat ih TYOO d 'n 's lee; plaat ih TOO d 'n 's lee), in a platitudinous manner.

platitudinize (plaat ih TYOO d' nize; plaat ih TOO d' nize), to utter platitudes.

plausible (PLAW zuh b'l) Originally this word meant worthy of approval or applause. Now it means *seeming* to be worthy, having the appearance of truth or reason; apparently worthy of confidence: *It seemed a plausible scheme for a quick return on investment, but he was inclined to proceed slowly before getting involved.* Something that is plausible strikes the superficial judgment favorably; it may or may not be deceptive: *They both felt the argument was plausible, but after analyzing it further they agreed it did not suit the position they were trying to defend.*

plausibly (PLAW zuh blee), in a plausible manner: *He presented his case plausibly.*

plausibility (plaw zuh BIL uh tee), the quality or state of being plausible. Also, **plausibleness** (PLAW zuh b'l n's).

poignant (POY n'nt; POY ny'nt) This comes from the same source as point and suggests sharpness as applied to the feelings. It means keenly distressing or deeply touching: *His most poignant memories were of the period of separation from his family;* or keenly appealing to the mind: *The poignant examples she gave won them over.*

poignantly (POY n'nt lee; POY ny'nt lee), in a poignant manner.

poignancy (POY n'n see; POY ny'n see), quality or state of being poignant: *the poignancy of her pleas.*

potential (puh TEN sh'l; po TEN sh'l) From the same source as potent, meaning powerful in actuality, this word differs in its sense of being capable of being powerful. It means possible as opposed to actual; capable of being or becoming: *It was apparent that the child was a potential musical prodigy.*

As a noun it means something that exists in a state of possibility: *His potential for further development looked promising.*

potentially (puh TEN shuh lee; po TEN shuh lee), not actually, but possibly: *He is potentially the greatest player the game has ever seen.*

potentiality (puh ten shee AAL uh tee; po ten shee AAL uh tee), possibility, potential state or quality: *The potentiality of war was always to be considered in the negotiations.*

practicable (PRAAK tuh kuh b'l) Capable of being put into practice or used, particularly in reference to the available means: *He was quite ingenious in working out a practicable way to transport the odd-shaped pieces of equipment.*

practicably (PRAAK tuh kuh blee), in such a way as to be practicable: *They decided the maneuver could be practicably executed.*

practicability (praak tuh kuh BIL uh tee), state or quality of being practicable; something practicable: *The location of the house presented some problems of practicability, because it was so far from transportation and shopping.*

Practicable is often confused with *practical,* which means sensible and businesslike as applied to persons, or efficient and workable as applied to things (*practicable* is used only of things, not of persons): *The plan was practical enough, but would be practicable only with the right personnel.*

pragmatic (praag MAAT ik) This word is from the Greek *pragmatikos,* active or skilled in law or business. It commonly means being concerned with practical consequences or values: *He employed pragmatic standards even in buying paintings, considering first whether they were likely to increase in value within a few years.* It is less frequently used to mean busy, active in affairs, usually with the implication of meddling or officiousness; conceited; opinionated. It also means pertaining to pragmatism, an American philosophical movement. The sense of having to do with the affairs of a state or community is no longer in common use except in the phrase *pragmatic sanction,* a decree handed down by a ruler and having the effect of fundamental law. Also, **pragmatical** (praag MAAT uh k'l).

pragmatically (praag MAAT uh k'lee), in a pragmatic manner: *She evaluated the alternatives pragmatically and decided the long-term advantages of one outweighed the more immediate benefits of the other.*

pragmatism (PRAAG muh tizm), a philosophical movement in which emphasis is placed on practical consequences and values as standards for interpreting philosophic ideas and as tests for determining their worth; also pragmatic character or conduct; officiousness, dogmatism; practicality.

pragmatist (PRAAG muh tist), one who adheres to the doctrines of pragmatism; or a busybody.

precarious (pruh KAIR ee 's) The Latin source word means obtained by plea or favor, hence the modern meaning of uncertain, insecure, dependent on circumstances beyond one's control: *She earned a precarious livelihood as an entertainer, wandering from place to place.* It may also suggest danger: *He kept a precarious balance on the narrow mountain path;* or insufficient foundation: *The precarious state of his bank balance would have worried his creditors, had they been aware of it.*

precariously (pruh KAIR ee 's lee), uncertainly, dangerously: *The cards were precariously arranged into a shaky structure.*

precariousness (pruh KAIR ee 's n's), quality or state of being precarious: *The precariousness of her position.*

precocious (pruh KO sh's) Ripening early, before maturity is usually expected; an adjective commonly applied to an early show of unusual talent or ability in children: *He was remarkably precocious in understanding complicated mathematical concepts before he was ten. A precocious display of brilliant piano technique by a girl of twelve thrilled the audience.*

precociously (pruh KO sh's lee), in a precocious manner.

precociousness (pruh KO sh's n's), early maturity or development: *The precociousness of his behavior startled those who did not know him.* Also, **precocity** (pruh KAHS uh tee).

premonition (pree muh NISH 'n; prem uh NISH 'n) From the Latin words meaning *before* and *warn*, this becomes a forewarning: *Various signs had given her a premonition that the outcome would be unfavorable.* It may be merely a feeling that something is about to happen, without conscious reason or evidence.

premonitory (pruh MON uh tawr ee), serving to warn beforehand: *She had premonitory twinges in her bones, indicating damp weather ahead.*

premonitorily (pruh mon uh TAWR uh lee), in a premonitory manner.

prerogative (prih RAHG uh t'v; pree RAHG uh t'v) An exclusive right or privilege attached to some office or position, as in the case of a ruler, or a person of high rank or authority: *To order a command performance is the prerogative of kings.*

As an adjective, the word means having, exercising, pertaining to, or existing by virtue of, a prerogative: *his prerogative powers*.

While a *privilege* is also a special advantage, it may be won by or bestowed on someone; *prerogative* implies an unquestioned right, without need to justify or account for.

prolix (PRO liks; pro LIKS) Extended to great, unnecessary, or tedious length, especially as applied to speaking or writing: *His reports were so prolix they had to be edited heavily to bring them down to manageable length for publication.*

prolixity (pro LIK sih tee), tediousness or undue lengthiness, especially in speaking or writing: *His prolixity was so well known that when he began to speak, half the audience settled down for a nap.* Also, **prolixness.**

prolixly (pro LIKS lee), in a prolix manner.

promulgate (pruh MUL gate; PRAHM 'l gate) To announce by open declaration, or proclaim formally, or put into operation, as a law, ruling, or decree. *A new amendment was promulgated at the convention.* It may also mean to set forth a theory or dogma or teach publicly, especially with the idea of gaining supporters: *St. Paul's great work was promulgating the teachings of Christ.*

promulgation (pro mul GAY sh'n; prahm 'l GAY sh'n), public declaration or official announcement; the act of promulgating: *The admiral was asked to resign because of his promulgation of doctrines considered detrimental to the service.*

promulgator (pro MUL gay t'r; PRAHM 'l gay t'r), one who promulgates, makes publicly or officially known.

propitious (pruh PISH's) Presenting favorable conditions, or favorably inclined: *The friendliness of the reception made him feel that the time was propitious for bringing up his new plan. It was propitious weather.*

propitiously (pruh PISH's lee), in a propitious manner: *Things seem to be working out propitiously.*

propitiousness (pruh PISH's n's), the quality or state of being propitious.

propitiate (pruh PISH ee ate), to make favorably inclined; appease or conciliate, particularly by admitting a fault and trying to make amends: *She realized how important it was to propitiate the more conservative members of the party if she was to be successful in her campaign.*

propitiator (pruh PISH ee ay t'r), one who propitiates.

propitiatingly (pruh PISH ee ay ting lee), in a propitiating manner.

propitiatory (pruh PISH ee uh tawr ee), conciliatory, intended to propitiate. Also, **propitiative** (pruh PISH ee uh tiv).

propitiation (pruh pish ee AY sh'n), the act of conciliation or appeasement, or something which propitiates: *She brought flowers by way of propitiation for being late.*

propitiable (pruh PISH ee uh b'l), capable of being propitiated.

Propitious is very similar in meaning to *auspicious* and *benign,* which also suggest favorableness. *Auspicious,* however, is slightly stronger in implying definitely favoring circumstances, while *propitious* has more of the feeling of the absence of unfavorable ones. *Benign* suggests a disposition to be favorable on the part of persons or agencies which have the power to exert an unfavorable influence.

quiescent (kwy ES 'nt; kwee ES 'nt) Related to quiet, this word means to be in a state of inactivity; to be still; suggests a temporary condition: *The dog lay quiescent in the sun, only twitching his tail when spoken to.*

quiescently (kwy ES 'nt lee; kwee ES 'nt lee), in a quiescent manner: *Exhausted by the long argument, she ended by accepting his conditions quiescently.*

quiescense (kwy ES 'ns; kwee ES 'ns), the state or quality of being quiescent: *There were periods of quiescense in the course of the disease.* Also, **quiescency** (kwy ES 'n see; kwee ES 'n see).

quintessence (kwin TES 'ns) In ancient and medieval philosophy, this was considered the fifth and highest essence or element—after earth, water, air, and fire—permeating the material world and composing the heavenly bodies. It was believed to be capable of being extracted, and thus came to mean the pure and concentrated essence of a substance, or the perfect embodiment of something: *Her walk was the quintessence of grace.*

quintessential (kwin tuh SEN sh'l), purest, having the quality of quintessence: *the quintessential romanticism of the poetry.*

quintessentially (kwin tuh SEN shuh lee), characterized by being quintessential: *The poetry was quintessentially romantic.*

quixotic (kwik SAHT ik) This is an adjective descriptive of qualities associated with Don Quixote, hero of the famous seventeenth century Spanish novel by Cervantes. Applied to persons, it means idealistic, extravagantly romantic, chivalrous, impractical: *He is of such a quixotic temperament he will plunge into any humani-*

tarian project without questioning its possible effectiveness. Applied to ideas, it means visionary, impracticable: *It is one of her quixotic plans to travel across the country to get an interview without even arranging for it in advance.* Also, **quixotical.**

quixotically (kwik SAHT ik 'lee), in a quixotic fashion.

quixotism (KWIK suh tizm), quixotic character or conduct, or idea or act. Also, **quixotry** (KWIK suh tree).

ramify (RAAM uh feye) The root of this verb is the Latin word for branch combined with a form of the verb to make. It means to divide or spread out into branches or branchlike parts. A nerve system or root system may be said to ramify. The word is also used of nonphysical things: *She hoped that once the central body was organized, it would ramify into many smaller groups and thus reach more people.*

ramification (raam uh fuh KAY sh'n), the act, process, or manner of branching out: *The ramification of the growth followed a pattern unfamiliar to the scientists who were studying it;* or an offshoot or branch from a main source: *Setting up a new office system led to more ramifications than he had expected.*

ramiform (RAAM uh form), branchlike or branched.

rapacious (ruh PAY sh's) This comes from a Latin word for greediness, which in turn derives from the verb meaning to seize and carry away; also the source of *rape.* This adjective means given to seizing for plunder or the satisfaction of greed: *rapacious raids in the surrounding countryside;* or excessively greedy: *her rapacious desire for jewels;* or, as applied to animals, living on prey: *Even a domestic cat retains some rapacious habits.*

rapaciously (ruh PAY sh's lee), in a greedy or preying manner.

rapaciousness (ruh PAY sh's n's), the quality or state of being rapacious: *His rapaciousness in art collecting was so well known that when he became interested in a painting his competitors withdrew.*

ravenous (RAAV uh n's) Extremely hungry: *They were ravenous when they returned from their hike;* craving food or satisfaction: *His demands for attention were so ravenous no one person could cope with him for long;* or rapacious; devouring eagerly.

ravenously (RAAV uh n's lee), in a ravenous manner, or to a ravenous degree: *He fell on the food ravenously, as if he hadn't eaten for days.*

ravenousness (RAAV uh n's n's), the quality or state of being ravenous: *the ravenousness of his appetite.*

Rapacious is almost synonymous with *ravenous* in conveying extreme greediness; but *rapacious* also suggests seizing the desired object. It implies greater intensity than *ravenous*. *Ravening* (RAAV uh ning) implies fierceness and savagery, especially in the manner of acquiring food. *Voracious* means devouring food greedily and in large quantity to satisfy an excessive appetite, or sometimes only for its own sake without regard for the degree of hunger.

recalcitrant (rih KAAL suh tr'nt) From the Latin word meaning to kick back, this adjective means resisting authority or control; stubbornly disobedient; *The recalcitrant child refused to leave the sandbox*. From this, it has also come to signify difficult to handle, unmanageable: *The recalcitrant mule was the despair of its driver*.

As a noun the word means one who is resistive or disobedient.

recalcitrance (rih KAAL suh tr'ns), resistance to authority or control, stubborn disobedience: *The recalcitrance of several States in defying the Supreme Court's decision*. Also, **recalcitrancy**.

recalcitrate (rih KAAL suh trate), to resist or oppose, show strong objection.

recalcitration (rih kaal suh TRAY sh'n), opposition or objection. These last two words are not commonly used in ordinary informal speaking or writing.

recapitulate (ree kuh PICH uh late) To review or summarize in orderly fashion, as at the end of a speech: *Now that I have heard your arguments, let me recapitulate*. In zoology this term means to repeat the stages of evolutionary development in the individual organism.

recapitulation (ree kuh pich uh LAY sh'n), the act or process of restating or summarizing: *She gave precise recapitulations of the two theories*. In the technical senses, in biology, the word refers to the theoretical repetition in the individual of the stages of development of its ancestors; in music, it is the third section of a movement, repeating the main theme, usually with some change.

recapitulative (ree kuh PICH uh lay t'v), related to or characterized by recapitulation: *It was largely a recapitulative assignment, calling for ability to organize*. Also, **recapitulatory** (ree kuh PICH uh luh tawr ee).

reciprocate (rih SIP ruh kate) The Latin root of this verb means to move back and forth, and this sense governs the modern meanings of the word and its derivatives. It may mean literally to move backward and forward, but the most common use is not in a physical sense but a figurative one, to give or feel in return, to interchange: *She reciprocated his love*. The implication is usually of equal return for something given, a correspondence of value or quality.

reciprocation (rih sip ruh KAY sh'n), the act or fact of reciprocating, a mutual giving and receiving: *The formal reciprocation of gifts by no means reflected a mutual affection*.

reciprocity (res uh PRAHS uh tee), a mutual exchange or reciprocation; especially an exchange of concessions, privileges, or courtesies between political units, institutions, or organizations: *Some states have reciprocity agreements to recognize without further examination the professional standing of doctors who have been medically qualified in their own states*. Also, **reciprocality** (rih sip ruh KAAL uh tee).

reciprocal (rih SIP ruh k'l), given, felt, or done by each of two parties to or for the other: *a reciprocal exchange of calls; reciprocal kindness*. There is an implied meaning of balance, exchange of equivalents. As a noun, it means something which has reciprocal relation to something else: *Responsibility is a reciprocal of privilege*.

reciprocally (rih SIP ruh k' lee), in a reciprocal manner, in return or exchange.

reciprocative (rih SIP ruh kay t'v), characterized by reciprocation, or serving to reciprocate.

reciprocator (rih SIP ruh kay t'r), one who reciprocates.

reciprocating (rih SIP ruh kay ting), moving back and forth, or having parts which move back and forth: *A pendulum is a reciprocating mechanism*. Also, **reciprocatory** (rih SIP ruh kuh tawr ee).

Reciprocal is sometimes used interchangeably with *mutual*. *Mutual* refers to something possessed, performed, or experienced by each of two or more, with respect to the others. But it cannot refer to physical things; *reciprocal* can: *a mutual friendship*, but *a reciprocal handshake*. Also, what is *mutual* must take place between two or more at the same time, while a *reciprocal* act need not be simultaneous with the ones it reciprocates.

recriminate (rih KRIM uh nate) The core of this word comes from the Latin verb meaning to accuse. It means to bring a countercharge against an accuser: *He recriminated by pointing out her own failures.*

recrimination (rih krim uh NAY sh'n), a counter accusation brought by the one accused: *He knew that as soon as he authorized the book's publication, there would be recriminations against him.*

recriminative (rih KRIM uh nay t'v), having the character of recrimination: *He reacted to the gossip by making recriminative remarks against those he believed to have started it.* Also, **recriminatory** (rih KRIM uh nuh tawr ee).

recriminator (rih KRIM uh nay t'r), one who accuses his accuser of a like crime.

rectitude (REK tuh tood; REK tuh tyood) *Recti-* is a word element meaning right or straight. The whole word means rightness of principle or practice: *His rectitude during his term of office, even in a generally corrupt administration, was no surprise to those who were familiar with his high moral principles;* or correctness: *the rectitude of his logic.*

redundant (rih DUN d'nt) The meaning of the Latin root is to overflow, to be in excess. This adjective means exceeding what is usual or natural, especially in using too many words to express an idea: *To her the repetitions and variations in the poem seemed subtle and charming; to him, redundant.*

redundancy (rih DUN d'n see), the state of being redundant: *The redundancy of his language gave it a Victorian quality;* or the superfluity itself: *One more testimonial speech would be a redundancy I could not tolerate.* Also, **redundance** (rih DUN d'ns).

redundantly (rih DUN d'nt lee), in a redundant manner.

reiterate (ree IT uh rate) To do or say over and over again, beyond the point of simple repetition: *A parent's capacity to listen to questions is hardly ever equal to a child's capacity to reiterate them.*

reiteration (ree it uh RAY sh'n), the act or process of reiterating: *Her mechanical reiteration of the finger exercises on the piano at last drove him out of the house;* repetition.

reiterative (ree IT uh ray t'v), marked by reiteration: *a reiterative pattern of speech.*

reiteratively (ree IT uh ray t'v lee), in a reiterative manner.

Repeat means to do or say something over again; *reiterate* implies insistent, often wearisome, repetition.

rejuvenate (rih JOO vuh nate) The *-juv-* shows the connection with *juvenile;* the word means to make young again, to restore to youthful vigor: *The fresh experiences of travel seemed to rejuvenate him.*

rejuvenation (rih joo vuh NAY sh'n), the restoration of youthful vigor, the state of being rejuvenated: *Dyeing her hair gave her a great sense of rejuvenation.*

rejuvenator (rih JOO vuh nay t'r), one who or that which rejuvenates: *the rejuvenator of the community.*

rejuvenescence (rih joo vuh NES 'ns), a renewal of youth, rejuvenation: *Her absorption in art seemed to stimulate a rejuvenescence.* This is slightly different from rejuvenation in conveying the sense of the process of becoming young again.

rejuvenescent (rih joo vuh NES 'nt), becoming young again, or making young again.

relegate (REL uh gate) From the Latin meaning to send back, this word means to send to some obscure position or place. It implies downgrading or getting rid of: *She relegated the unwelcome visitors to the least attractive guest room.* It also means to assign a matter for consideration: *Much of the important work of Congress is relegated to subcommittees;* or to refer something to a particular class or kind: *They agreed to relegate this matter to the heading of new business on the agenda.*

relegation (rel uh GAY sh'n), removal to some lesser place or condition: *his relegation to the office of third vice-president;* assignment: *the relegation of the painting to the surrealist collection.*

relegable (REL uh guh b'l), capable of being relegated. This is somewhat awkward to use, and is not often heard or seen.

Because of the similarity of sound and the sense of "assign" which they have in common, *delegate* may be confused with *relegate. Delegate,* however, means to assign functions to another as an agent or deputy; *relegate* is merely to assign a matter for consideration.

repartee (rep 'r TEE) From a French word meaning an answering thrust (a fencing term), this is a quick and witty reply. More broadly and in common use, the meaning is talk characterized by quickness and wittiness of reply: *Their repartee so entertained the party that all other conversation stopped;* or skill in making witty replies: *His gift for repartee was the delight of his friends and the terror of his enemies.*

Riposte (ri POST) is also a fencing term, a quick thrust after parrying a lunge, and like repartee can apply to conversation. It is a clever retort, but neither as light nor as witty as *repartee*.

requisite (REK wuh zit) As an adjective, this means required by the nature of things or by circumstances: *She has the requisite physical qualifications for modeling*. As a noun it means a necessary thing, something required: *Her dressing table was crowded with toilet requisites*.

requisiteness (REK wuh z't n's), the quality or state of being necessary: *The requisiteness of the equipment he asked for was obvious*.

requisition (rek wuh ZISH 'n), the act of requiring or demanding, especially a formal or official demand for something to be done, given, or provided: *You will have to fill out a requisition before you are given any supplies*.

As a verb this means to require or take for use, press into service: *The commander requisitioned all the medical supplies in the village*.

As an adjective, *requisite* is similar to necessary and essential in the sense of something vital for the fulfillment of a need. *Necessary* implies something which cannot be done without, or which is an inevitable consequence of something else: *It is necessary that these things be done in a certain order*, a necessary evil. *Essential* is a stronger word, since it means of the essence, absolutely vital: *the essential ingredient; It is essential that you do not miss that train*. *Indispensable* suggests that which cannot be omitted, neglected, or removed without changing the nature or quality of the condition being dealt with: *His presence is indispensable to our plan*.

As a noun, *requisite* is almost synonymous with *requirement* (both come from the same Latin root); but *requirement* implies something demanded according to fixed external standards: *job requirement;* while *requisite* implies what is necessary according to the nature of things or circumstances, rather than to any outside imposition of regulations: *She had all the requisites of a successful hostess*.

rescind (rih SIND) To take back, annul, or revoke; usually applied to some formal ruling or document, as an order, law, or contract: *A referendum was required to rescind the amendment. The general would not rescind his order*.

resilient (rih ZIL y'nt) This is a literal translation of the Latin source word, meaning rebounding, springing back, returning to the original form after being bent or stretched. It may be applied to things: *Rubber is a resilient material;* and by extension, to people: *Her resilient disposition never lets her remain depressed for long.*

resilience (rih ZIL y'ns), the power to spring back: *The resilience of Germany has been one of the most remarkable economic phenomena since World War II;* elasticity, rebound: *The resiliency of the ball made out of the new synthetic was much greater than he had expected.* Also, **resiliency** (rih ZIL y'n see).

resiliently (rih ZIL y'nt lee), in a resilient manner.

retaliate (rih TAAL ee ate) ſo pay back in kind, especially injury or evil, usually for revenge: *Each time she felt she was snubbed, she retaliated by spreading malicious rumors.*

retaliation (rih taal ee AY sh'n), the act of retaliation, the return of like for like: *A fundamental principle of gang life is retaliation for every real or imagined injury, trespass, or insult.*

retaliatory (rih TAAL ee uh tor ee), of the nature of retaliation: *retaliatory tactics.* Also, **retaliative** (rih TAAL ee ay t'v).

Retaliate is similar to *reciprocate* in the idea of returning in kind, but the latter is a more neutral word, applicable to any kind of act or feeling. *Retaliate* includes the element of injury and the motive of revenge, and applies only to actions.

reticent (RET uh s'nt) Disposed to be silent; not inclined to speak freely; reserved: *Although he was reticent about his personal life, he was always talkative about office matters.*

reticence (RET uh s'ns), the quality or state of being reticent; reserve; or an instance of being reticent: *Her usual reticence melted a little under the influence of the admiration.*

reticently (RET uh s'nt lee), in a reserved manner.

reticulate (rih TIK yuh late) To form into a network: *His object was to reticulate the wires to form a model of what the larger construction would be.*

As an adjective, (rih TIK yuh l't) it means netlike, or covered with a network: *The leaves exhibited a reticulate pattern of veins.*

reticulation (rih tik yuh LAY sh'n), a network, or the formation, arrangement, or appearance of a network: *The painting looked to him like nothing but a reticulation of fine lines in drab colors.*

reticular (rih TIK yuh l'r), another adjective meaning the same as reticulate, but with the additional sense of intricate or entangled: *the reticular structure of the nest.*

All of these words derive from the Latin *reticulum,* little net, which is also the source of *reticule,* a kind of drawstring bag which women used to carry as a purse. Originally of mesh, it was later made of other materials. The *reticle* of optical instruments is also from this source; it is a system of fine lines, dots, or cross hairs in the eyepiece of a sight, telescope, or other optical instrument to help place the object in focus.

rigorous (RIG uh r's) The Latin *rigor* means stiffness, hardness; this adjective, meaning severe, harsh, carries the sense of undeviating inflexibility. It may be applied to persons: *The governing board was rigorous in its application of the rules;* things, especially weather: *a rigorous winter, a rigorous school;* or abstract ideas, usually having to do with conduct or standards: *She insisted on rigorous etiquette in her household.*

rigor (RIG 'r), strictness, severity, harshness: *the rigor of his self-discipline; rigor of mathematical formulas; the rigor of military life. Rigor mortis* is literally the stiffness of death, the stiffening of the muscles which sets in after death.

rigorousness (RIG uh r's n's), state or quality of being rigorous: *the rigorousness of the course.*

rigorously (RIG uh r's lee), in a rigorous manner: *He held them rigorously to the original outline.*

rigorism (RIG uh rizm), extreme strictness in behavior and principle, especially in matters of ethics or morals. In Roman Catholic theology, it is the principle that in doubtful cases of conscience, the strict course is always to be followed. It is not often found in informal usage.

rigid (RIJ id), from the Latin word meaning to be stiff, is like *rigorous* in the sense of being stiff or unyielding, but does not necessarily convey the same degree of hardship or severity. Also, it may apply to concrete things: *a rigid stem; a rigid structure,* which rigorous does not.

saccharine (SAAK uh rin; SAAK uh rine) The first two syllables are a combining form signifying sugar. The word means of a sugary sweetness, hence excessively sweet: relating to, or of the nature of sugar; overly or falsely sweet: *his saccharine greetings to the guests; saccharine calendar art.* The word for the tablets widely used as a sugar substitute is saccharin, without the final *-e.*

saccharinely (SAAK uh rin lee; SAAK uh rine lee), in a saccharine manner.

saccharinity (saak uh RIN ih tee), the quality or state of being excessively sweet: *Her saccharinity of tone in talking to the children both amused and annoyed the parents.*

sacrosanct (SAAK ro saankt) Especially sacred or inviolable. The quality of extreme holiness is conveyed in the combination of the two parts: *sacro-* comes from a Latin word meaning sacred, *-sanct* from one meaning to make holy.

sacrosanctity (saak ro SAANK tih tee), the quality or state of being sacrosanct: *the sacrosanctity of the relics.*

Sacred also applies to things entitled to veneration because of association with religious purposes, deities, or with divinity, but, unlike sacrosanct, it need not be restricted to such use. It may also mean reverently dedicated to some person or object: *a sacred memory;* or secured against violation by respect for human rather than divine authority: *the sacred rights our forefathers fought for.*

salient (SAY lee 'nt) The literal meaning of the Latin source is leaping or springing, and this is one meaning of the word today. Another, which derives from it, is projecting or pointing outward, as an angle, beyond a general line or level. The figurative meaning, thus, is prominent or conspicuous: *One of his salient characteristics was his love of children. The salient points of an argument are seldom examined.*

As a noun it means a projecting angle, especially one that juts out from a bastion or from a battle line: *They were satisfied that the salient offered no weak spot to the enemy.*

salience (SAY lee 'ns), physical prominence or projection; conspicuousness, striking feature: *The salience of the tree in the foreground overshadowed the gardens that lay behind it.* Also, **saliency** (SAY lee 'n see).

saliently (SAY lee 'nt lee), strikingly, outstandingly.

sanguine (SAANG gwin) The origin of this word, which means naturally cheerful and hopeful, confident, is in the Latin word for blood. It also means relating to blood, and blood-red. In the old physiology, in which the body was believed to be dominated by one of four humors, each of which produced a characteristic temperament, the sanguine one was that in which blood predominated. It was thought to be responsible for the ruddy complexion, sturdiness, and the general high spirits associated with this kind of personality. Thus the word has come to apply to the optimism of this type of temperament: *He took a sanguine view of the prospects.* Also, **sanguineous** (saang GWIN ee 's), although this is not common.

sanguinely (SAANG gwin lee), hopefully, optimistically.

sanguineness (SAANG gwin n's), the quality or state of being hopeful, confident: *The audience found it hard to accept the sanguineness of his speech in the face of the discouraging newspaper reports.*

There are many other words with the combining form *sanguin-*, but the meanings of the others have to do directly with blood.

sardonic (sahr DAHN ik) Bitterly ironical, sneering, mocking. One who is sardonic takes a cynical view of human motives. He may convey his attitude by his expression or by what he says: *His sardonic remarks were obviously intended to upset her.*

sardonically (sahr DAHN uh k'lee), in a sardonic manner, with a sardonic attitude: *He viewed the antics of the tourists sardonically for what he considered their lack of sophistication.*

sardonicism (sahr DAHN uh sizm), sardonic quality or attitude: *His sardonicism usually amused her, but when the bitterness was unrelieved by humor, it infuriated her.*

Sarcastic, sardonic both mean ironic, but *sardonic* conveys more fundamental bitterness and cynicism. *Sardonicism* represents a point of view, *sarcasm* a device.

scintillate (SIN tih late) To emit sparks, sparkle, flash; may be used in a literal sense: *The hammered metal scintillated in the sun;* or a figurative one: *Her wit scintillated under the stimulation of an appreciative audience.*

scintillation (sin tih LAY sh'n), the act of scintillating, a spark or flash: *the scintillation of the jewels;* in astronomy, the twinkling motion of the light of the stars.

scintillant (SIN tih l'nt), scintillating, sparkling.

scintilla (sin TIL uh), a spark, a minute particle or trace. This is usually used in the figurative sense, and in a negative phrase: *There seemed to be not a scintilla of hope.*

sedentary (SED 'n tair ee) From the Latin verb meaning to sit, this means characterized by or requiring a sitting posture: *The doctor said she could do only sedentary work;* accustomed to sitting or taking little exercise: *It was hard for him to overcome the sedentary habits of his long convalescence.*

sedentarily (sed 'n TAIR uh lee), in a sedentary manner: *He preferred to take his recreation sedentarily.*

sedentariness (SED 'n tair ee n's) the quality or state of being sedentary: *Her inclination to sedentariness at an age when most children are very active worried her family.*

sedulous (SEJ uh l's) sounds like sedentary, but it means diligent in application or attention, persevering: *her sedulous polishing of the furniture;* persistently or carefully maintained: *sedulous devotion to the cause.*

serenity (suh REN uh tee) Calmness or tranquility: *the serenity of her disposition in the face of trouble and grief;* clearness, as of the sky or air: *The serenity of the day made very detail in the garden stand out clearly.* When the word is preceded by *his* or *your* and capitalized, it is a title of honor given to certain reigning princes. Also, **sereneness,** except in the last sense.

serene (suh REEN), calm, peaceful, tranquil: *Her serene manner emphasized her dignity;* clear, fair: *serene climate.* The adjective is also used in the titles of certain princes and important figures, in which case it is capitalized: *His Serene Highness.*

serenely (suh REEN lee), in a serene manner: *serenely self-assured.*

simultaneous (seye m'l TAY nee 's; sim 'l TAY nee 's) Existing, occurring, or operating at the same time: *Although thunder and lightning are simultaneous, the lightning appears to be first because the speed of light is greater than that of sound. There will be simultaneous showings of the new movie in selected cities all over the country.*

simultaneously (seye m'l TAY nee 's lee; sim 'l TAY nee 's lee), in a simultaneous manner, at the same time: *They began to talk simultaneously; then each asked the other to speak first.*

simultaneousness (seye m'l TAY nee 's n's; sim 'l TAY nee 's n's), the quality or state of being simultaneous: *The simultaneousness of the explosions in different parts of the city made it unlikely that they could be unrelated accidents.* Also, **simultaneity** (seye m'l tuh NEE uh tee; sim 'l tuh NEE uh tee).

sinecure (SEYE nuh kyoor; SIN uh kyoor) A job or position requiring little or no work, especially one providing profitable returns: *Political patronage always consists of a certain number of sinecures as well as legitimate jobs.* This general meaning comes from the specific British reference, still current, to a churchly office with income attached (such as a rectory) but without cure of souls—that is without responsibility for the parishioners' spiritual care. This in turn is from the Latin phrase, *sine cura,* without care.

solicitous (suh LIS uh t's) Anxious or concerned over something (followed by for, about, of, or a subordinate clause): *solicitous* *about every detail of the journey; solicitous for her comfort;* anxiously desirous: *solicitous of the goodwill of his neighbors.*

solicitously (suh LIS uh t's lee), in a solicitous manner.

solicitude (suh LIS uh tyood; suh LIS uh tood), a state of anxiety or concern: *Her friend's solicitude during her illness was touching;* excessive attention or assistance caused by anxiety: *One would have thought from his solicitude over the arrangements for the party that it was the most important event of the year.* Also **solicitousness** (suh LIS uh t's n's).

solicit (suh LIS it), the verb from which the other forms derive, means to seek for by plea, earnest or respectful request, or formal application: *He solicited their attention for a statement of their position.* It usually implies a sense of urgency or personal interest, or an attempt to influence.

solicitor (suh LIS uh t'r), one who solicits, usually for business, contributions, etc. In Britain, it refers specifically to the member of the legal profession who advises clients, represents them in the lower courts, and prepares cases for barristers to try in the higher courts, where solicitors themselves are not qualified to appear.

solicitation (suh lis uh TAY sh'n), the act of soliciting: *solicitation of funds;* entreaty, urging, or petition: *His solicitation of her good offices in interesting other people in the project was successful.*

sonorous (suh NAWR 's; SAHN 'r 's) Giving out, or capable of giving out, a sound, especially a deep full sound: *the sonorous ring of the brass gong; the canyon sonorous with echoes;* rich or full in sound, as in language or verse: *the sonorous roll of Milton's poetry.* The second meaning pertains to high-flown expression, excessively ornamented to give the effect of impressiveness: *sonorous oratory.*

sonorously (suh NAWR 's lee; SAHN 'r 's lee), in a sonorous manner: *His low notes rang out sonorously.*

sonority (suh NAWR uh tee), the condition or quality of being resonant or sonorous: *The sonority of his voice filled the hall; the sonorities of the verse.* Also, **sonorousness** (suh NAWR 's n's).

spontaneous (spahn TAY nee 's) This means coming from a natural personal impulse, without effort or forethought or holding back: *a spontaneous expression of pleasure; the spontaneous quality that comes through in her writing.* The idea of naturalness and freedom from external forces also appears in the meaning of growing naturally, or produced by natural processes (as opposed to cultivation), or rising from internal forces: *An apparently spontaneous growth of a plant new to the area was noted in several different places along the river this year.*

spontaneously (spahn TAY nee 's lee), in a spontaneous manner: *She spontaneously offered to help, and almost immediately wished she hadn't.*

spontaneity (spahn tuh NEE uh tee), the state, quality, or fact of being spontaneous: *The spontaneity of the applause was flattering.* Also, **spontaneousness** (spahn TAY nee 's n's).

sporadic (spaw RAAD ik) The meaning of the modern word and the Greek word from which it comes is the same: scattered. It most often signifies something scattered in time; appearing or happening at intervals, or irregularly: *sporadic fires, sporadic outbreaks of a new dance craze;* may also refer to irregular or separated instances in space: *There were sporadic appearances of the disease in several parts of the city.* Also, **sporadical.**

sporadically (spaw RAAD uh k'lee), in a sporadic manner.

sporadicalness (spaw RAAD uh k'l n's), the quality or state of being sporadic. Also, **sporadicity** (spaw ruh DIS uh tee).

Sporadic and spasmodic (spaaz MAHD ik), are both characterized by irregularity. But *spasmodic* comes from spasm, a sudden, violent, abnormal muscular contraction, and means pertaining to or like a spasm, sudden and violent, but brief, occurring at intervals, without smoothness or continuity: *spasmodic movement, spasmodic growth.*

spurious (SPYOOR ee 's) The Latin word *spurius* means of illegitimate birth, hence its current meaning of not from the right, reputed, or pretended source; false, not genuine or true: *spurious claims to the inheritance; a spurious appearance of age in counterfeit antiques.*

spuriously (SPYOOR ee 's lee), falsely, in a spurious manner: *He spuriously assumed royal titles in order to enter circles where he would not otherwise have been welcome.*

spuriousness (SPYOOR ee 's n's), falseness, the state or quality of being spurious: *She was satisfied that the spuriousness of her jewels could have been detected only by an expert.*

strategic (struh TEE jik) Generally, pertaining to skillful management in getting the better of an opponent or attaining an end: *the strategic planting of rumors to discredit the opposition;* specifically, relating to the art or science of employing the means of war in planning and directing large military operations: *stra-*

tegic placement of artillery; or important in such ope. tions: *The strategic point for both sides was the hill that commanded a view of the sea.* Also, **strategical** (struh TEE juh k'l).

strategically (struh TEE juh k'lee), in a strategic manner: *He placed himself strategically so as to be able to watch both exits.*

strategy (STRAAT uh jee), the use of devices and materials of war in planning military operations, or the method of conducting such operations: *The strategy was to mass the ships in the harbor to remind the natives of their availability;* skill in accomplishing an end or outwitting an opponent: *His years of experience had made him a master of political strategy.*

strategist (STRAAT uh jist), one experienced in strategy.

strenuous (STREN yoo 's) Applied to persons, this means vigorous, energetic, enthusiastically active: *She is a strenuous promoter of any kind of cultural program;* applied to actions, life, efforts, it means characterized by vigorous exertion, with a suggestion of urgency: *strenuous participation in sports; strenuous pursuit of a hobby; strenuous objections.*

strenuously (STREN yoo 's lee), in a strenuous manner.

strenuousness (STREN yoo 's n's), the quality or state of being strenuous: *the strenuousness of the campaign; strenuousness of one's efforts.* Also, **strenuosity** (stren yoo AHS ih tee).

suavity (SWAH vuh tee; SWAAV uh tee) A smoothly agreeable quality: *The suavity of his charm reflected many years of polishing his manners and conversation in sophisticated circles. We loved the suavity and richness of the furnishings.* There is sometimes a suggestion that the quality is superficial or slick. Also, **suaveness** (SWAHV n's; SWAVE n's).

suave (SWAHV; SWAVE), smoothly pleasant or polite, characterized by practiced agreeableness: *suave assurance in dealing with objections.*

suavely (SWAHV lee; SWAVE lee), in a suave manner, smoothly.

supercilious (soo per SIL ee 's) Supercilium means eyebrow, and there is perhaps a connection between the raised eyebrow as an expression of disdain and the meaning of this word, haughtily disdainful or contemptuous: *her supercilious manner; a supercilious critic.*

superciliously (soo per SIL ee 's lee), in a patronizing or haughty manner: *He rejected the request superciliously, as if no one but a fool would have made it.*

superciliousness (soo per SIL ee 's n's), the quality or state of being disdainful or contemptuous: *Although his ability was* *recognized, his superciliousness was a drawback to his advancement.*

surreptitious (ser up TISH 's) This is from a Latin word meaning to snatch away secretly. It means secret, unauthorized, obtained by or acting in a stealthy way: *They would have starved during the enemy occupation if he had not had surreptitious ways of procuring food; a surreptitious conversation; surreptitious removal of small amounts of cash from time to time.*

surreptitiously (ser up TISH 's lee), in a stealthy manner, in an unauthorized way: *He took an apple from the bowl surreptitiously, as he was not allowed to have fruit.*

surreptitiousness (ser up TISH 's n's), stealthiness, secretive behavior: *It was a long time before his surreptitiousness in sneaking out was discovered.*

There is no connection between this word and *repetitious*.

susceptible (suh SEP tuh b'l) Capable of receiving, admitting, undergoing, or being affected by something (followed by *of* or *to*): *The great dramatic roles are susceptible of several interpretations. Is this animal susceptible to control?* It implies being open to: *susceptible to respiratory infections;* or impressionable: *She was always susceptible to an appeal to her position in the community.*

susceptibly (suh SEP tuh blee), in a susceptible manner: *She responded susceptibly to his flattery, as he knew she would.*

susceptibility (suh sep tuh BIL uh tee), state or character of being susceptible: *susceptibility* to *bribery;* capability of being easily affected. In the plural, it means capacities for emotions, sensitive feelings: *One always had to be careful not to injure her susceptibilities.* Also, **susceptibleness** (suh SEP tuh b'l n's).

sycophant (SIK uh f'nt) A self-seeking flatterer: *Any person of wealth or importance can expect to be plagued by sycophants hoping to gain some advantage from the association.* In slang, he'd be an apple-polisher.

sycophantic (sik uh FAAN tik), fawning, toadying, characteristic of a sycophant: *sycophantic flattery.* Also, **sycophantical** (sik uh FAAH tuh k'l).

sycophantically (sik uh FAAN tuh k'lee), in a sycophantic manner.

sycophancy (SIK un f'n see), self-seeking or toadying flattery: *His sycophancy was obvious to everyone but his victim;* the character or behavior of a sycophant.

synthesis (SIN thuh sis) The Greek word means a putting together; the modern meaning is the same, a combination of parts or elements into a complex whole: *a synthesis of chemical compounds, a synthesis of the prevailing ideas of the period;* a process of reasoning from general assumptions or principles to conclusions or specific instances.

synthesize (SIN thuh size), to make up by combining parts or elements; to combine into a complex whole: *It was difficult to synthesize the various notes into a coherent paper.*

synthetic (sin THET ik) as an adjective means pertaining to, proceeding by, or involving synthesis: *It is at best a synthetic work—a summary of what others have done rather than an original one.* In chemistry it refers to compounds produced by chemical reactions in a laboratory, as opposed to those of natural origin. From this sense it has expanded to mean pertaining to any artificial process used to imitate or approach natural conditions: *A number of synthetic devices were used in training to simulate actual battle conditions.* It has gone even beyond this to the additional sense of artificial, therefore unnatural or false, distorted: *a synthetic smile; synthetic flowers; synthetic standards of conduct.* Also, **synthetical** (sin THET uh k'l). As a noun it means something made by a synthetic or chemical process: *Synthetics have almost taken over the clothing industry.*

synthetically (sin THET uh k'lee), in a synthetic manner: *Since it has been possible to produce certain drugs synthetically, many diseases which used to be fatal have been brought under control.*

The opposite of *synthesis* is *analysis,* the separation of a whole, either material substance or matter of thought, into the elements which compose it.

temperament (TEM per uh m'nt; TEM pruh m'nt) The physical organization peculiar to an individual which permanently affects his way of thinking, feeling, and acting; the natural disposition: *He was melancholy by temperament.* Temperaments may be lively, sluggish, nervous, serene. The word has also come to mean an unusual personal makeup, marked by peculiarities of behavior or feeling, and disinclination to submit to ordinary rules and restraints: *Artists are often thought to have a peculiar and distinctive kind of temperament which makes them suffer under ordinary conventions.*

temperamental (tem per uh MEN t'l; tem pruh MEN t'l), having or showing a strongly marked individual temperament: *He had a temperamental aversion to solicitude;* moody, irritable, or sensitive: *Her temperamental outbursts were a source of distress and annoyance to her fellow workers.*

temporize (TEM puh rize) The first two syllables, showing the relationship to words like *tempo* and *temporary,* suggest that this word also has to do with time. It means to gain time or delay matters by acting indecisively or evasively: *He tried to keep the conversation on minor matters, temporizing until his brother could get there to deal with the major ones.* It also means to yield ostensibly or temporarily to the current of opinion or circumstances: *A successful politician must be prepared to temporize;* to come to terms with or effect a compromise.

temporizer (TEM puh reye z'r), one who temporizes: *She did not want to deal with him because he had a reputation as a temporizer, and she wanted to make plans within the week.*

temporizingly (TEM puh reye zing lee), in a temporizing manner: *She felt he was acting temporizingly in putting off the interview until next week.*

tenacious (tuh NAY sh's) From the Latin verb meaning to hold, this means characterized by keeping a firm hold: *tenacious of possessions;* having a great capacity to retain: *tenacious memory;* persistent or obstinate: *his tenacious devotion;* adhesive, sticky, holding together: *The new glue was so tenacious, I could not pull the two pieces apart.*

tenaciously (tuh NAY sh's lee), in a tenacious manner: *He defended his theory tenaciously.*

tenacity (tuh NAAS uh tee), the quality or state of being tenacious; determination: *tenacity of purpose;* persistence: *tenacity in working out repeated experiments;* cohesiveness: *tenacity of the structure;* adhesiveness: *The paper stuck to the wood with great tenacity.* Also, **tenaciousness** (tuh NAY sh's n's).

terminology (ter muh NAHL uh jee) The *term-* with which this word begins shows the relation to the idea of names. Term is a word or phrase naming something; terminology is a system of terms in a particular area of knowledge: *musical terminology.*

terminological (ter muh nuh LAHJ uh k'l), relating to terminology: *They became so involved in a terminological argument that they never reached the subject at issue.*

terminologically (ter muh nuh LAHJ uh k'lee), in a terminological way: *Terminologically, he was correct, but artistically he might have chosen a better word.*

therapy (THAIR uh pee) The treatment of disease, as by application of remedies or by a process of cure: *Warm water baths and massage are often prescribed as therapy for polio;* a curative power or quality: *The arrival of her father acted as therapy.* In recent years the term has expanded beyond the purely medical to take in the treatment of mental disease and personal maladjustment: *psychoanalytic therapy;* and even broader ills, including the social: *Person-to-person contact with people of other countries and races is one of the best forms of therapy for prejudice.*

therapist (THAIR uh pist), one who practices therapy, such as a doctor, or one trained in applying remedies for the cure or rehabilitation of patients physically or mentally.

therapeutic (thair uh PYOO tik) is almost the Greek form of the word from which all these derive, meaning, in the original, attending or treating medically. The modern meaning is pertaining to the treating or curing of disorders: *Within a few days the therapeutic effect of the change of climate was apparent.* Also, **therapeutical** (thair uh PYOO tuh k'l).

therapeutically (thair uh PYOO tuh k'lee), in a therapeutic manner.

therapeutics (thair uh PYOO tiks), the branch of medicine concerned with the remedial treatment of disease.

tirade (TEYE rade; tuh RADE) A prolonged outburst against someone or something, intense in feeling and immoderate in expression: *He retreated under a tirade of abusive language, out of all proportion to the offense.* It comes from a word meaning to draw or shoot, and still has the suggestion of a volley of shot, or an attack.

tortuous (TAWR choo 's) Full of twists, turns, or bends, as applied to physical things: *a tortuous path, tortuous shapes;* or to processes: *The tortuous logic by which he reached his conclusion would scarcely bear examination.* The second sense sometimes suggests a lack of straightforwardness, or intentional deceit: *He had such a tortuous way of asking that they did not realize until he actually said so that he was asking for money.*

tortuosity (tawr choo AHS uh tee), state of being tortuous, twisted form or course, crookedness: *The tortuosity of the road provided interesting views but quickly exhausted them. His intellectual processes exhibited such tortuosity the others soon lost the thread of his argument.* Also, **tortuousness** (TAWR choo 's n's).

tortuously (TAWR choo 's lee), in a tortuous manner: *The stream meandered tortuously.*

Tortuous, torture, and *torturous* have the same source, but they are related in meaning only in sharing the sense of twisting. It is possible to say that a course is *torturous,* meaning that it is a painfully twisted one.

travesty (TRAAV is tee) A humorous treatment of a serious work or subject, with intent to ridicule and usually debase: *A feature of the annual banquet was a travesty on some of the political issues of the past year;* a debased likeness or imitation: *The portrait of Dorian Gray was a horrible travesty on his outward appearance.*

As a verb it means to turn something serious to ridicule by burlesque imitation or treatment, or to imitate grotesquely or absurdly: *The article travestied the play's excesses so mercilessly that the Little Theater committee decided they could not risk putting it on.*

trepidation (trep ih DAY sh'n) This comes from a Latin word meaning to tremble. It means nervous (that is, trembling) alarm or agitation. It is fear with the connotation of timidity: *She approached the meeting with his parents with trepidation, not knowing what to expect.*

Other forms of this word are *trepid, trepidant, trepidate,* and *trepidity,* but they are seldom used. The negative form of the adjective, however—*intrepid* (in TREP 'd), meaning fearless—is in common use.

tumultuous (tyoo MUL choo 's; too MUL choo 's) Characterized by or causing uproar, disorderliness, disturbance: *tumultuous waterfall; tumultuous crowds;* disturbed or agitated, as the mind or feelings: *his tumultuous emotions on hearing the news.*

tumultuously (tyoo MUL choo 's lee; too MUL choo 's lee), in a tumultuous manner, boisterously, noisily, agitatedly: *The children responded tumultuously to the suggestion of an excursion.*

tumult (TYOO m'lt; TOO m'lt), the commotion or disturbance of a large crowd, usually accompanied by noise: *He was able to quiet the tumult merely by appearing on the balcony;* a popular outbreak or uprising: *Tumult erupted at the unwelcome announcement;* mental or emotional agitation: *Whenever he saw her unexpectedly, he was thrown into a tumult.*

tumultuousness (tyoo MUL choo 's n's; too MUL choo 's n's), storminess, disorderliness, uproar: *the tumultuousness of the waves.*

turbulent (TER byuh l'nt) Characterized by or inclined to disturbances, disorder, or insubordination: *turbulent sea, turbulent youth, turbulent mob;* disturbed, agitated: *With great effort, he gained control of his turbulent feelings*.

turbulence (TER byuh l'ns), state or quality of being turbulent; agitation, unruly conduct: *the turbulence of conditions with war threatening*. The word also has the special meteorological meaning of irregular motion of the atmosphere, as indicated by rapid changes in wind speed and direction: *The pilot announced that some turbulence was to be expected over the mountains;* or (hydraulics) the irregular secondary motion due to eddies within a fluid. Also, **turbulency** (TER byuh l'n see).

turbulently (TER byuh l'nt lee), in a turbulent manner.

This word is very close in meaning to tumultuous, but the latter has more of a sense of noisiness and riotousness; *turbulent,* of insubordination or unrest.

turgid (TER jid) Literally this means swollen: *a turgid abscess on his finger;* figuratively, then, it means inflated or pompous, referring to language or style: *the turgid prose; turgid style of writing*.

turgidity (ter JID ih tee), condition of being swollen or inflated: *turgidity around the ankle-joints, the turgidity of his oratory*. Also, **turgidness**.

turgidly (TER jid lee), in a turgid manner.

turgescent (ter JES 'nt), becoming swollen, swelling: *The area around the insect bite was turgescent*.

turgescence (ter JES 'ns), the state of becoming swollen. Also, **turgescency** (ter JES 'n see).

ulterior (ul TEER ee 'r) The first two syllables are from the Latin *ultra,* beyond, and the word means beyond what is seen or expressed, intentionally kept concealed: *He had an ulterior purpose in making the suggestion;* coming at a later time or stage: *ulterior development;* or situated beyond, or on the farther side: *the ulterior expanse of meadow*. These latter two senses are not nearly as commonly employed as the first one.

ulteriorly (ul TEER ee 'r lee), in an ulterior manner, characterized by being ulterior.

ultimate (UL tuh m't) From the Latin *ultimus,* the last or farthest, every sense of this adjective implies final limits. It means forming the final aim or object: *His ultimate purpose in employing a variety of teaching devices was to improve the* reading level for that grade; coming at the end of an action or process, decisive: *He was training a successor with a view to his own ultimate retirement from business responsibilities;* fundamental, indicating a point beyond which it is impossible to go: *the river's ultimate source, ultimate boundaries, ultimate truths;* or the last of a series: *This will be the ultimate experiment.*

As a noun it is the final point, the utmost: *She had extended herself to the ultimate—she could do no more;* a fundamental fact or principle: *Science is always trying to approach the ultimate.*

ultimately (UL tuh m't lee), finally, fundamentally: *Ultimately he will have to make the choice. All colors can ultimately be analyzed into some combination of the primary ones.*

ultimatum (ul tuh MAY t'm), a final proposal or statement of conditions: *He gave his partner an ultimatum: to sell out to him or buy him out.* More specifically, it applies to diplomatic relations: a proposal made by one party, which, if rejected by the other may lead to a break in relations, or even war.

ultimateness (UL tuh m't n's), the state or degree of being ultimate: *The ultimateness of his decision was not to be questioned.*

unctuous (UNK choo 's) The Latin source of this word means ointment; this adjective means having the quality of ointment— that is, greasy or oily. It may refer to physical things: *unctuous to the touch; Certain minerals are unctuous in feeling;* more commonly applied to manner or behavior in an unfavorable way, suggesting excessive or affected smoothness. It is usually associated with hypocrisy or pretense: *His unctuous concern for her comfort made her suspicious, for she hardly knew him;* hypocrisy with regard to religious or spiritual matters: *His unctuous, high moral tone annoyed his hearers, who were aware of the shabby way he treated his family.*

unctuously (UNK choo 's lee), in an unctuous manner: *The unctuously flattering introduction made the speaker most uncomfortable.*

unctuousness (UNK choo 's n's), the state or quality of being unctuous: *The unctuousness of his voice and manner captivated a succession of foolish, elderly widows, who believed they were being courted by a well-to-do man of the world.* Also, **unctuosity** (unk choo AHS uh tee).

unction (UNK sh'n) is specifically the act of anointing, especially for religious or medical purposes; or something soothing or comforting. From this it has taken on the meaning of a soothing, sympathetic, or persuasive quality in speaking or discussion, particularly on religious subjects; and from this into the sense of unctuousness—that is, a professional, conventional, or affected earnestness or fervor.

unmitigated (un MIT uh gay t'd) To mitigate is to lessen in force or intensity, to moderate the severity of anything distressing. Unmitigated, therefore, is not softened or lessened: *Her sorrow was unmitigated by any gleam of hope;* or unqualified, absolute: *unmitigated stubborness.*

unmitigatedly (un MIT uh gay t'd lee), in an unmitigated manner: *He was unmitigatedly opposed to any relaxation of the rules.*

utilitarian (yoo til uh TAIR ee 'n) Clearly showing its derivation from utility, usefulness, or something useful, this means pertaining to utility, or being useful, having regard to usefulness rather than beauty or decorativeness: *Utilitarian though it was in accomplishing the purpose, she felt it need not have been quite so ugly;* one who believes in the principles of utilitarianism: *To a utilitarian, buying paintings and going to concerts was sheer extravangance.*

utilitarianism (yoo til uh TAIR ee 'n izm), the belief that virtue is based on usefulness, and that conduct should be directed toward producing the greatest happiness for the greatest number: *As an adherent of utilitarianism, he felt that the good of the town would be best served by removing the few families living on the site considered most desirable for the new school.*

vacillate (VAAS uh late) To sway unsteadily or stagger, hence to waver in the physical sense: *His weakness caused him to vacillate back and forth as he tried to make his way along the path;* more commonly used of mental uncertainty or lack of firmness: *He vacillated so long in making a decision that he finally lost the opportunity.*

vacillation (vaas uh LAY sh'n), irresolution, wavering in mind or opinion: *He was surprised at her vacillation about accepting the offer because she was usually so quick to make up her mind;* unsteady movements.

vacillating (VAAS uh lay ting), wavering, given to variability in feelings or judgments: *Her vacillating emotions left him uncertain of where he stood with her from one day to the next.* Also, **vacillatory** (VAAS uh luh tor ee).

vacillatingly (VAAS uh lay ting lee), in an uncertain or irresolute manner.

validity (vuh LID uh tee) From the Latin word meaning strong; a derivative of valid; soundness, justness having force or authority: *the validity of his arguments, the validity of his assumptions;* legal force: *As a witness he was able to testify to the validity of the document.* Also, **validness** (VAAL 'd n's).

validate (VAAL uh date), to confirm: *He explained how his experiments validated the theory;* give legal force to: *The new ordinance served to validate the informal agreements under which they had previously operated.*

validation (VAAL uh DAY sh'n), an act or process of confirming or legalizing: *A stamp was required as evidence of validation of the document.*

variegate (VAIR ee uh gate; VAIR uh gate) The relationship to variety and varied appears in the first part of this word. It means to make varied in appearance, as by marking with different colors, etc.: *She showed the children how to variegate the Easter eggs by dipping them in different dyes;* to give variety to: *He variegated the effect in the garden by the arrangement of plants of different heights and colors.*

variegated (VAIR ee uh gay t'd; VAIR uh gay t'd), varied: *a variegated assortment;* marked with spots or patches of different colors: *The variegated quilt was an outstanding example of its kind.*

variegation (vair ee uh GAY sh'n; VAIR uh GAY sh'n), the state or condition of being variegated, varied coloration: *The variegation of the pattern was too confusing to be attractive;* or the act of variegating.

venerate (VEN uh rate) To regard someone or something with deep respect or reverence, usually because of nobility, tradition, or age: *He venerated his old teacher.*

veneration (ven uh RAY sh'n), reverence: *their veneration for the bishop;* the act of venerating, or the state of being venerated: *She received the veneration of her subjects;* expression of reverent feeling: *She bowed her head as a gesture of veneration.*

venerable (VEN uh ruh b'l), the related adjective, makes clearer the association of respect and age. It means ancient, or commanding respect or interest by reason of age, dignity of appearance, or associations.

versatile (VER suh t'l) The source of this word is the Latin verb meaning to turn, and accordingly this means capable of turning easily from one thing to another, hence adaptable, many-sided in abilities: *He was so versatile in sports that he had offers from baseball, basketball, and football teams;* having many uses or applications: *a versatile plastic; a versatile suit.*

versatilely (VER suh t'lee), in a versatile manner: *He handled his assignments so versatilely that he soon earned a promotion.*

versatility (ver suh TIL uh tee), the quality, or state of being versatile; capability of turning from one thing to another: *She showed remarkable versatility in producing excellent work in several different art forms.*

These words do not imply flightiness or instability, but aptitude and ability—qualities worthy of admiration.

vicarious (veye KAIR ee 's; vih KAIR ee 's) The meaning of vicar as a representative or substitute for another gives a clue to this word, which means done or received in place of another: *Many parents enjoy vicarious satisfactions through their children;* acting for or substituting for another: *She felt a heavy responsibility in her vicarious role as head of the family.*

vicariously (veye KAIR ee 's lee; vih KAIR ee 's lee), by means of, or like a substitute: *She had to accept the award vicariously. He suffered vicariously throughout her long illness.*

vicariousness (veye KAIR ee 's n's; vih KAIR ee 's n's), the quality or state of being vicarious: *The necessary vicariousness of her pleasures, handicapped as she was, did not seem to diminish her enjoyment.*

vicissitude (vih SIS uh tood; vih SIS uh tyood) A change or variation, or something different, occurring in the course of a thing; successive alterations, change or succession of one state or thing to another. It is more often used in the plural than the singular: *The vicissitudes of life often cause dramatic changes in the conditions of individuals—and in their politics.* The idea of change of luck or accident of fortune now generally suggests an unfavorable turn, a difficulty or hardship: *They were exhausted by the vicissitudes of the journey. They had to overcome many unforeseen vicissitudes during their long separation.*

vicissitudinous (vih sis uh TOOD uh n's; vih sis uh TYOOD uh n's), characterized by or filled with vicissitudes: *a vicissitudinous project, marked by delays and mishaps.* This adjective has a literary flavor, and is not commonly used.

vigilance (VIJ uh l'ns) Watchfulness, especially with regard to danger; alertness: *Even the vigilance of the border guards could not prevent a few alarming incidents.*

vigilant (VIJ uh l'nt), keenly attentive to detect danger, constantly watchful: *A vigilant watchman*.

vigilantly (VIJ uh l'nt lee), in a vigilant manner: *On receiving the report of a threatened kidnaping, the police patrolled the neighborhood vigilantly*.

In the United States, *vigilance committee* has the special meaning of an unauthorized group of citizens organized to maintain order and punish crime in the absence of regular or efficient courts, as in a situation of pioneer conditions. A member of such a committee is a *vigilante* (vij uh LAAN tee).

All of these words come from *vigil,* a watch kept by night or other times; a period of watchful attention; or a keeping awake for any purpose during the normal hours of sleep.

vindictive (vin DIK t'v) The Latin *vindicta* means revenge; this word is an adjective meaning revengeful, showing a revengeful spirit: *Her vindictive remarks about her mother-in-law were embarrassing to all those present*.

vindictively (vin DIK t'v lee), in a vindictive manner: *She vindictively reported him to the teacher when he would not stop annoying her*.

vindictiveness (vin DIK t'v n's), the quality or state of being vindictive: *His well-known vindictiveness in competition brought an element of added danger to the fight*.

vindicate (VIN duh kate), which ultimately comes from the same source as *vindictive,* and originally meant to avenge or punish. it later took on the meaning of delivering or setting free from something, as a charge or suspicion or dishonor: *His conduct alone seemed to vindicate him from the unsupported accusations;* to afford justification for, uphold or defend: *The results completely vindicated his judgment. Milton's purpose in "Paradise Lost" was to vindicate the ways of God to man. Vindication* is a defense or justification. *Vindicatory* (vin duh kuh tawr ee) means serving to vindicate: *vindicatory articles;* or punishing: *The sentence was a vindicatory rather than a deterrent one; vindicatory* combines the ideas of justification and revenge. *Vindicable* (vin duh kuh b'l) is another adjective, meaning capable of being vindicated: *That statement is not vindicable by any law of logic*.

vitiate (VISH ee ate) To make the quality or substance of something defective or faulty, to spoil or corrupt: *His insistence on gratitude vitiated his generosity. Her affected manner of speech only vitiates the good impression she is trying to make;* to invalidate: *The absence of the proper signature vitiates the document.*

vitiation (vish ee AY sh'n), the quality or state of being vitiated: *The vitiation of all his worthy purposes;* or the act of vitiating: *His partner's refusal to accept the terms constituted a vitiation of their business relationship.*

vitiator (VISH ee ay t'r), one who vitiates.

vociferous (vuh SIF uh r's) Crying out noisily and insistently: *the vociferous shouts of his supporters;* of the nature of loud outcry: *The newspapers are vociferous in their demands for action.*

vociferously (vuh SIF uh r's lee), in a vociferous manner: *He defended himself vociferously against the attacks of his opponent in debate.*

vociferousness (vuh SIF uh r's n's), the quality or state of being vociferous: *the vociferousness of his arguments.*

vociferate (vuh SIF uh rate), to cry out loudly or noisily: *He could hear the angry women vociferating in the street below.*

vociferation (vuh sif uh RAY sh'n), noisy outcry, the act of vociferating: *the vociferation of the recital of her injuries.*

voluminous (vuh LOO muh n's) This comes from a Latin adjective meaning full of folds, which in turn derives from the word for a roll of papyrus or parchment—that is, a book. Thus, the word volume contains both meanings, a book, or a mass or large quantity. Voluminous, then, means filling, or capable of filling, a large volume or book: *voluminous works; voluminous notes;* of great size, extent, or fullness: *a woman of voluminous figure; a voluminous record collection; voluminous curtains.*

voluminously (vuh LOO muh n's lee), in a voluminous manner: *He wrote so voluminously, it was a burden to try to keep up the correspondence.*

voluminousness (vuh LOO muh n's n's), the state or quality of being voluminous: *The voluminousness of her skirt was an embarrassment in the high wind.* Also, **voluminosity** (vuh loo muh NAHS uh tee), although this form is not so common.

voluptuous (vuh LUP choo 's) The Latin *voluptas* means pleasure, and this adjective means characterized by or tending to serve pleasure, particularly luxurious or sensuous enjoyment: *He took great voluptuous satisfaction in wine and women, much less in song;* suggestive of an inclination to sensuous pleasure: *a voluptuous figure.*

voluptuously (vuh LUP choo 's lee), in a voluptuous manner: *His neighbors suspected him of indulging himself voluptuously during his frequent absences.*

voluptuousness (vuh LUP choo 's n's), the quality of being voluptuous. Also, **voluptuosity** (vuh lup choo AHS uh tee), not very common.

voluptuary (vuh LUP choo air ee), as a noun, one who is given up to luxurious or sensuous pleasures: *He would have enjoyed the existence of a voluptuary, but his means did not permit it.* As an adjective, it means pertaining to or characterized by such pleasures: *voluptuary inclinations.*

vulnerable (VUL nuh ruh b'l) Capable of being hurt, in a physical sense: *particularly vulnerable to blood infections; their vulnerable position on the hill;* otherwise open to attack or damage: *The circumstances of his bankruptcy made him vulnerable to a series of accusations. He was vulnerable to temptation.*

vulnerably (VUL nuh ruh blee), in a vulnerable manner: *vulnerably exposed.*

vulnerability (vul nuh ruh BIL uh tee), capability of being injured, openness to attack or damage: *Knowing his vulnerability to the influence of a stronger personality, his mother was vigilant in choosing proper companions for him.* Also, **vulnerableness** (VUL nuh ruh b'l n's).

whimsical (HWIM zuh k'l) From whimsy, an odd or fanciful notion, this means given to such notions: *a whimsical impulse to go out to the lake cottage in mid-winter;* or of an odd, quaint, or comical kind: *Lewis Carroll's whimsical verse; a whimsical costume for the carnival.*

whimsically (HWIM zuh k'lee), in a whimsical manner: *She whimsically caricatured several of their acquaintances.*

whimsicality (hwim zuh KALL uh tee), whimsical character: *Her painting has a whimsicality which is charming;* a whimsical notion, act or speech: *The apparent whimsicality of the president's decision disturbed the members.* Also, whimsicalness (HWIM zuh k'l n's).

Whimsy itself comes from *whim,* an odd notion or a freakish fancy or desire. It carries a sense of impulsiveness and of response to mood rather than reason.

zenith (ZEE n'th) The point in the sky vertically above any place or observer, or the highest point in the sky reached by a heavenly body: *The sun was approaching its zenith.* From this meaning has come the sense of the highest point or state, the peak: *Shakespeare represents the zenith of Elizabethan literature.*

Nadir (NAY d'r; NAY deer) is the opposite of *zenith* in both senses. It is the point in the celestial sphere vertically beneath any place or observer; or the lowest point of anything: *the nadir of the curve; the nadir of his misfortunes.*

Authoritative Guides to Better Self-Expression:

Word power made·easy with
The Ballantine Reference Library